D0168321

BETTER
THINKING
&
REASONING

BETTER
THINKING
REASONING

Ron Tagliapietra

Bob Jones University Press
Greenville, South Carolina 29614

Library of Congress Cataloging-in-Publication Data

Tagliapietra, Ron, 1956-
   Better thinking and reasoning / Ron Tagliapietra.
     p.   cm.
   Includes bibliographical references and indexes.
   ISBN 0-89084-831-9
   1. Logic.   2. Reasoning.   I. Title.
BC108.T24   1995   95–40058
                                         CIP

Better Thinking and Reasoning
by Ron Tagliapietra

Edited by Debbie L. Parker
Cover by Sam Laterza

© 1995 Bob Jones University Press
Greenville, South Carolina 29614

ISBN 0-89084-831-9

15   14   13   12   11   10 9 8 7 6 5 4 3

Contents

To the Teacher

Studying logic may seem difficult, but it will be rewarding. Students usually profit from subjects in proportion to the effort expended. If little is expected, little is received. A unit or course on logic can challenge and discipline the student's mind in a way that will benefit him in his other courses of study.

Though the rewards are great, time constraints vary. To help meet your needs, we have tried to make the text flexible. You may use this text in any of the following five ways: (1) resource, (2) supplementary unit, (3) study skills course, (4) logic course, or (5) independent study. Suggestions for implementing each of these purposes follow.

As a Resource for Other Specific Courses

You can use topics, applications, or verses from this book in your course at relevant points, or you can cover one chapter as a unit.

History, Speech, and English—Material from Chapters 1-3 can be discussed briefly. Chapters 6, 10, and 11 (skip formal fallacies in Chapter 11) will require a day each. Skip most of the applications except as follows. For history, use mainly the history applications (Chapters 2 and 11). For speech, treat the history applications as speech assignments and discuss the debate (Chapter 1) and news (Chapter 3) applications as examples of problems in giving rebuttals in debate. For English, treat the history, debate, and news applications as examples of written work for an English class. You can also discuss the English grammar application in Chapter 6 (and Questions 6-7) if you so desire.

Science—On a single day, help students see the importance of creating and clarifying terms in science (Chapter 1), defining by characterizing (Chapter 2), and using true statements (Chapter 3).

Skip the applications in the text for those chapters. Cover Chapters 6 and 8 in detail including the science application sections. If desired, mention the material on weak inductions (proper methods misused) from Chapter 10. Chapter 8 presents key concepts for science students, and do not overlook Questions 1-6 in that chapter.

Mathematics—In math as in science, several comments from Chapters 1-3 will be relevant. Other relevant chapters will be easier if a student has been (or is being) introduced to truth tables from a geometry course. Chapters 4-5 provide considerable work with truth tables so as to supplement a unit on them in a geometry course. Likewise, Chapters 7 and 9 explain reasoning techniques and provide practice with proofs in the context of logic instead of geometry. Cover the formal fallacies of Chapter 11 and the tools of Chapter 12 (including Venn diagrams). Stress the math applications in Chapters 7 and 12. Also, consider using the computer (Chapter 5) and logic (Chapters 7 and 9) applications.

As a Supplementary Unit

You can present a three-to-six-week unit in a science, history, speech, language, or writing class.

Cover the chapters below briefly and select questions to assign as homework. Use days 5, 10, and 15 for catch-up or review. If you have more than three weeks, expand the time allotted for the more difficult topics (Chapters 6, 8, and 10) or cover extra material from Chapters 11 and 12.

Day(s)	Chapters
1	Introduction
2	1
3	2
4	3
5	Review or catch up
6-7	6 (and first paragraph of 7)
8-9	8
10	Review or catch up
11-12	10

13-14	11 (skip formal fallacies; assign Questions 3-4, 8-9 only)
15	Review or catch up

As a Study Skills Course

Some schools may offer a short course on study skills to prepare students for college or standardized tests. The schedule below will work for a teacher who presents well-organized summaries, discusses some applications, and assigns memory verses and selected questions as homework. Days 10, 20, and 30 are for catch up or tests. Many teachers of this course will prefer to spend twice as long on each chapter to create a semester-long course.

Day(s)	Chapters	Applications
1	Introduction	
2	1	Tests
3-4	2	History
5-6	3	
7-9	4	Tests
10	Review or catch up	
11-12	6	English, science
13-16	7	Tests, math
17-19	8	
20	Review or catch up	
21-22	10	Business
23-25	11	History
26-28	12	Math
29	Afterword and review	
30	Review or catch up	

As a Logic Course

A course on logic should cover the entire book. This will probably require a semester. Discuss all topics, applications, Bible applications, and memory verses. Assign most of the questions (a couple each day) and hold students accountable for memory verses.

Week	Chapters
1	Introduction and 1
2	2
3	3
4	4
5	4-5
6	5
7	6
8	7
9	7-8
10	8
11	9
12	10
13	11
14	11-12
15	12 and Afterword

As an Independent Study

If a student works through the book on his own, he should be taking high school geometry or have already taken it. A background in geometry will prepare him mentally for this kind of challenge. Set the pace according to the logic course schedule (or adapt the study skills course schedule to your time schedule).

Introduction

Do You Need Better Thinking and Reasoning?

Have you ever been misled by a well-meaning person? Sometimes people make statements that they think are true but which turn out to be partially or completely false. Those who believed the original statements are hurt in the process. These situations, even when they aren't malicious, hurt just the same. Every person influences others and is accountable for his statements. In light of this, you should desire to use clear words, truthful statements, and reasonable arguments, and to see through deceptions.

Clarity, truthfulness, and reasonableness are all qualities of God. God has declared His Word clearly in Jesus (John 1:1-14); He is truth itself (John 14:6) and reason itself (see *logos* in John 1:1). He has neither deceived nor been deceived; He is not the author of confusion (I Cor. 14:33).

Furthermore, He expects these qualities in His people.

1. Use clear words, "Let your yea be yea" (James 5:12), and like Paul, "use great plainness of speech" (II Cor. 3:12). In fact you will be judged for "every idle word" (Matt. 12:36).

2. Speak the truth—both "in love" (Eph. 4:15) and with all men (Eph. 4:25).

3. Give good reasons. Use "sound speech, that cannot be condemned" (Titus 2:8). Do things "decently and in order" (I Cor. 14:40).

4. Do not be deceived. "Let no man deceive you by any means" (II Thess. 2:3, also Eph. 5:6). Let no "man spoil you through philosophy and vain deceit" (Col. 2:8), but instead search "the scriptures daily, whether those things were so" (Acts 17:11).

God has also given you examples to follow in Jesus and the apostles. Jesus silenced the Jews with strong arguments on numerous occasions (four times in Matt. 22 alone). In Acts it is said, "And Paul, as his manner was, went in unto them, and three sabbath days reasoned with them out of the scriptures" (Acts 17:2). Not only did Paul reason with them for three weeks, but that was what he *always* did everywhere he went ("as his manner was"). In fact, Acts describes how Paul was "opening and alleging" (17:3), how "he reasoned in the synagogue every sabbath, and persuaded the Jews and the Greeks" (18:4), and again how he was "disputing and persuading" (19:8). Similar statements are made of Paul in Acts 17:17, 18:11, 18:19, and 19:9.

Why study thinking? God's character reflects orderly reasonable thinking, His Word commands it, and Jesus and Paul exemplify it. Any one of these reasons would be enough. Yet there are more reasons. It is important for you to understand the Bible, yet the Bible includes many arguments. Besides those that Jesus made, Peter refutes the scoffers (II Pet. 3), Paul refutes the Judaizers (Gal. 3-5) and the Gnostics (Col. 2). Paul also argues many points of doctrine (Rom. 3-8, I Cor. 15, Eph. 2). John's whole gospel is to argue the facts so that we might be saved (John 20:30-31). Without good thinking skills many of God's messages to you will appear to be "partly cloudy" if not "dense fog."

Thinking skills are not limited to the understanding of the Bible. Everyone constantly depends on words, factual statements, arguments, and counterarguments—in school, at home, at work, and in church. Look at the following examples.

School
English: Give the theme of *War and Peace*. Support your position with instances (cite page numbers).
History: What positive consequences did the Vietnam War have? Explain your view.
Math: Prove the Exterior Angle Theorem.
Business: Using costs from the last ten years, estimate the costs for the company for next year.
Bible: What is the biblical position on television? Prove your view from Scripture.
Science: Identify this chemical using tests. Write your experiment based on the scientific method. Identify each conclusion.

Home
Why should you borrow the car?
What is wrong with working at a lounge to help pay for college?
Why does my brother get to go to camp and I don't?
Why is the baby crying?

Work
Why should you be given a raise?
Why is the new budget better than the old?
What is wrong with Positive Mental Attitude Seminars?
Is a business partnership proper?

Church
What reasons can I give someone to believe Jesus?
How much should I give to the church? Does the Bible give me a
   principle for giving?
What is the best way to reach our neighborhood—should we begin
   a bus ministry?

Each of these questions can be tricky. Improper reasoning on your part can result in poor grades, strife at home, financial loss, or a poor testimony. Good thinking is essential to every area of your life.

How Do You Get Better Thinking and Reasoning?

Developing any skill takes both practice and perseverance. To be a good athlete, both strong muscles and their coordination are necessary. A great weight lifter may or may not be a good football player, but it is certain that no matter how well coordinated a man is, he will not make it in football without developing some strength. The coach can assign coordination and strength-building drills, but the player must accept the responsibility for exercising and practicing the drills.

In the same way, thinking requires facts and their coordination. The key in an argument may be a fact that does not interest you. You need to *know* a *lot* about a lot of things. The first thing you can do to be a good thinker is to get excited about learning. If you are in school, listen attentively and read each textbook diligently. If you are not in school, turn off the television and read. Read actively by outlining or taking notes. These basic drills of thinking will help you throughout life.

The next thing you can do is to let this book be your coach for coordinating the facts. Remember, though, the coach cannot make an athlete in a night. Persevering practice in the weight room and running in ankle weights seem unrelated to the game. It's hard work, but it's only the start. To coordinate their muscles, players must practice the plays over and over again for speed and accuracy. The best players continue to run drills in their free time. By analogy, the book can coach you, and the questions provide some drills, but it is up to you to practice and develop the skills. Apply proper reasoning in classes, while reading, and even in casual conversation. By following these suggestions, you will better analyze problems, draw conclusions, and avoid errors in the use of your facts.

The first two chapters identify the role of *words*. Effective use of words is the first step since every argument uses them. Some arguments hinge on a single word. In Matthew 22:31-33, the key word is "AM" as contrasted to "was." Thus, these two chapters develop your ability to choose words carefully.

Words combine to form sentences, so Chapters 3, 4, and 5 discuss *sentences* and *truth values*. As you study true and false sentences, develop an appreciation for truthfulness. Get the facts straight.

Sentences combine to support or defend main points. This means that if you know correct lines of argument, you will use them more successfully. Chapters 6 through 9 analyze *arguments* to help you properly draw conclusions from the facts.

A knowledge of common mistakes should help you to avoid them. Chapters 10 and 11 classify common *fallacies*. Being alert for common errors is an aid toward the goal of not being deceived. The final chapter, Chapter 12, will help you expand and synthesize these tools of thinking.

Each chapter will include concepts, applications, summary, and questions. Concepts are the hardest but are the most important. They are the keys to the material. The applications demonstrate how the material is practical. Be sure to learn the memory verse in the application section so that God can conform your reasoning to His. The conclusion and list of terms in each chapter summarize key points for you to review and make sure you understand. The questions are included to offer practice for developing each reasoning "muscle." The questions permit the book to be used as a text or supplement, but more importantly, they enable you to check to see if you understand the concepts.

Chapters 4, 5, 7, and 9 will be the hardest for most people. In many ways they are the most important. Treat them as opportunities for practice and perseverance. They are the ankle weights in this drill, and if you slow down while reading them, then it just shows that muscles are building!

It is our prayer that those who persevere will find rich reward. The coach often says, "No pain, no gain," and we too will say it to encourage you. You will get out of the chapters (especially the hard ones) and the questions only as much as you put into them. God makes promises to the diligent that should encourage you even more than the coach's slogan.

"The hand of the diligent shall bear rule: but the slothful shall be under tribute" (Prov. 12:24).

"The soul of the sluggard desireth, and hath nothing: but the soul of the diligent shall be made fat [blessed]" (Prov. 13:4).

May the Lord strengthen you through your study.

Purposes of Definition

A dictionary definition is useful when you need to know what a word means. Is that the only time when a definition is helpful? Actually, there are four purposes for definitions.

Concepts

Characterizing—By far, **characterizing** is the most familiar purpose for definition. Dictionary definitions are descriptive. They characterize the way people use a word. Characterizations are either accurate or inaccurate depending on whether the word usage is correctly conveyed. Many words have more than one meaning. In this case *all* meanings must be listed. The word *trunk,* for instance, may be used to refer to elephants, trees, cars, torsos, suitcases, and swimsuits. A dictionary must explain these uses and correctly describe each. The intended meaning of the word in a sentence is determined by context.

Creating—The purpose of **creating** meaning can be achieved by coining a new word or adapting an old word to a new use. When telephones were invented, words were needed to refer to the object and its parts. Someone coined the term *telephone,* and a new word was added to the English language. This happens more often than you may think. Words are coined for new inventions, ideas, laws, and brand names. Even your peer group coins words that have meaning among your friends! When you coin a word, you create a new word. Sometimes, though, instead of creating a new word, you may create a new meaning for an old word. *Disk* has been in the English language for centuries; however, its use in the context of recorded music is a more recent development. The music industry needed a new word for the invention; instead of creating an entirely new word like *fluje,* they created a new meaning for the existing word *disk.* When the music industry extended the meaning of disk, they created a new meaning. If you began to use the word *fluffy* among your friends to refer to things you like, you would be extending meaning too.

Clarifying—When you give a word a specialized meaning in a particular context, you are **clarifying** the definition. For instance, if a teacher tells you to turn in neat homework, you may print neatly and turn it in. The teacher may have expected it to be typed. He could clarify his requirements this way—"All work is to be neat. For purposes of this class, *neat* means typed without erasures or manual corrections, margins not more than 1 1/2 inches wide, and a title page should also be included." This type of definition designates a usage of a term and makes specific the intent for a given context. Courts clarify the meaning of *safe* in laws about pollution, drinking and driving, and substances found in foods.

Convincing—Words are basic to your effectiveness in making a point. If a person agrees that *sin* is breaking God's laws, he is more likely to agree that he has broken them and needs salvation than if he believes that *sin* is just behavior that hurts someone else. When definitions are provided for arguing a point, the purpose for the definition is usually **convincing.** Politicians define *overspending* to get your vote, and commercials define *household needs* to get your purchase. It is important to think about what the speaker is promoting and whether the definition is acceptable. At times, it may be scientific research that uses such definitions. Physicists once defined atoms as the smallest particles. This definition pointed the way to further research. When atoms were split, the definition proved to be faulty. This example shows that such definitions can be helpful guides, but they must be considered carefully.

Applications

Knowing the purposes of definition can help you detect frauds in business, excel in writing and speaking, answer true-false quizzes, and understand the Bible. These are just a few of the benefits of this study. After reading these examples, see if you can think of any more.

Debate—Whether in a political debate, a classroom debate, or in the subtle advertising techniques of commercials, you will see the convincing type of definition everywhere. This type of definition is very successful in commercials. Many people laugh at a commercial that is very one-sided, but they buy the product at the store because they remember the brand name (and the laugh) instead of the poor reason to buy it. You can build sales resistance by identifying the bias in the definition. Evaluating definitions can also help when a debate on abortion is assigned in class. The antiabortion side will not win by *defining* abortion as murder because the other side will never agree to such a loaded definition. Instead, a common ground must be found for the term; then clear evidence must be presented to prove from the definition that it constitutes murder. Compromise of conviction is not necessary, but tactful presentations, clear communication, and an even temper are required. When a definition seems loaded, you can be sure that its purpose is to convince.

   Business—The word *average* has many meanings. Its characterization includes the mean (usual computation of average value), mode (most frequent value), and median (middlemost value). On a simple level imagine that a company has five employees: three stock boys, a salesman, and a president. The president makes $53,000 a year, the salesman $19,000, and the stock boys $9,000, $9,000, and $10,000 (one has worked there longer). The mean income is $20,000 per year [($53,000 + $19,000 + $10,000 + $9,000 + $9,000) ÷ 5]. The mode is $9,000 (it occurs twice), and the median is $10,000 (two people higher, two lower). Now if the president reports a $20,000 *average* salary per year (using the mean), he has not lied, but his bragging is misleading since only one person earns that much. On the other hand, he may report a $9,000 average (using the mode) if he wants to put on a humble act of "not making very much" (even though *he* is)! To be honest, he should specify which kind of *average* he used. Since there were only a few (under 30) employees, the median is the most honest average for annual salaries. Averages of just a few numbers are best reported by medians. Knowledge of averages should alert consumers to seek more information when they hear about a great *average*. These kinds of consumer tips help you develop sales resistance and avoid losing money in frauds.

   Test-taking—True-false questions often require knowledge of definitions. Consider this test item: "All parallelograms are trapezoids." True or false? The answer to this question depends upon which book you read. Each textbook must choose between the two possible definitions that follow.

1. A trapezoid is a quadrilateral with exactly one pair of parallel sides.
2. A trapezoid is a quadrilateral with at least one pair of parallel sides.

A geometry course that uses the first definition has the advantage of being able to refer to separate categories without confusion but has the disadvantage of having to prove over again for parallelograms every statement proved for trapezoids. Since each definition has an advantage and a disadvantage, not all writers prefer the same one.

This does *not* mean that you can answer the true-false question whichever way you want! Every time you read a math book, you must carefully check which definition the author and your teacher are using. Your answer will be true or false in the context of your class. (It should be false for definition 1 and true for definition 2.)

Bible—The term *inspired* is another good example of the importance of word definitions. Today people say that the *Iliad* was inspired, or that a scientist had an inspiration, or that an opera was inspiring. It is important to know that when we say those things we mean only that Homer or the scientist had a good idea, or that the opera either was food for thought or was emotionally exciting. On the other hand, the word *inspiration* when applied to Scripture does not mean that some men had a great idea and sat down to write the Bible. Instead, Scripture tells us that "men of God spake as they were moved [carried along] by the Holy Ghost"(II Pet. 1:21). All men who wrote Scripture, including Paul and Peter, were carried along like a ship driven by the wind. They were infallibly guided so that the Scriptures have exactly the right wording. In fact, the phrase "were driven" in Acts 27:17, describing Paul's storm-tossed ship, translates the same Greek word translated "moved" in II Peter 1:21. The Greek word translated "inspiration" in II Timothy 3:16 is a brand new Greek word (that is, it does not appear in earlier Greek literature). The new term combines two Greek words which together mean God-breathed, telling us that God breathed out His Word. Creating a word to put inspiration on a divine instead of a human level shows how important definitions can be. These Scriptures prove that the biblical statement "All scripture is given by inspiration of God" refers to God's act, not to human creativity.

Memory Verse—Matthew 12:36
"But I say unto you, That every idle word that men shall speak, they shall give account thereof in the day of judgment."

The verse above shows that words are important because God commands carefulness with words. If the words of man are important, how much more important are God's Words! In the previous section you saw the importance of correctly understanding the word *inspiration*. In fact, in Bible study you must seek to properly understand each word.

God also explains that His Word is important. Mark 13:31 says that "Heaven and earth shall pass away: but my words shall not pass away" (also see Matt. 24:35 and Luke 21:33). God's Word is eternal. In Matthew 5:18, Jesus says, "One jot or one tittle shall in no wise pass from the law, till all be fulfilled." Jots and tittles are parts of letters. This means that not only are the word meanings important but also the choice of words down to the spelling is important! God's Word is very exact.

Jesus also gave an example of the importance of the meaning of a word. Previously, you read about His argument with the Sadducees in Matthew 22:30-33 (see the Introduction). Do you remember that His support for life after death was based on the word *am* in a verse in the Old Testament (Exod. 3:6)? Just one word was enough to end the discussion.

Conclusion

According to the Bible, words are important. You have looked at four specific words and their definitions: *average, inspiration, trapezoid,* and *abortion.* Since each word means different things to different people in different contexts, you must carefully seek out the author's intended meaning. Notice how each word was defined for a different purpose. These words illustrate the four purposes for definition: characterizing, creating, clarifying, and convincing.

The word *average* is characterized by three different (but similar) meanings. This can cause confusion. Care must be taken to avoid being misled.

The word *inspiration* was given a newly created meaning in the Bible. Since there was no word for God's unique method of writing the Bible, God explicitly gave a definition to avoid confusion.

The term *trapezoid* is clarified in each math book for the context of the course. Two definitions are possible and equally valid, but not at the same time.

The term *abortion* is often defined and used to provoke emotional reaction. This causes the actual facts of the discussion to be ignored. To avoid this, when your purpose is *convincing,* try to find a neutral meaning for the term and then use good evidence to make your point.

No one likes it when someone twists his statements. Therefore, you should show other people the courtesy that you desire by understanding their statements with the meaning they intended. You will understand their statements better if you keep in mind the purpose of their definitions.

Terms

    characterizing
    clarifying
    convincing
    creating

Questions

1. Which purpose for definition is illustrated by each definition below?

    a. In this class, *light* is any electromagnetic wave with a frequency between 10^{14} and 10^{16} hertz (cycles per second).

    b. The word *fork* means (1) a multiple pronged implement for eating food or transporting hay, (2) two parts, (3) to pass or to hand over.

    c. For purposes of the National Park Service, *campsite* includes any spot at which one or more persons can sleep and/or cook.

    d. A *fintop* is a hair style in which a strip of long hair down the center of the head is treated to stand straight up, while the rest of the untreated hair is clipped short.

    e. A *smoker* is a person who rudely and habitually pollutes the air and becomes prone to lung cancer.

2. From the following list select the best definition for *socialism*.
   a. the Soviet Dream
   b. government interference with the workers' salaries
   c. a system of government which has economic equality as a goal
   d. a system of government which protects the rights of the poor
   e. a system of government which punishes diligence and rewards sloth
3. Bible definitions
   a. Which purpose for definitions can be found in Adam's naming of the animals in Genesis 2:19-20?
   b. How is God's love defined in John 3:16? Which purpose does God display in this definition?
4. What reasons have been presented in the text as the biblical basis for the importance of words?
5. Choose a word in each group to define. Try to write a good definition and then compare yours to a dictionary or Bible dictionary as appropriate.
   a. propitiation, redemption, or atonement
   b. depression, economy, or recession
6. Choose the name of a Christian denomination (Baptist, Presbyterian, etc.).
   a. Find the dictionary characterization. Did the dictionary succeed in stating it in a neutral manner?
   b. Consult a Christian dictionary or handbook of denominations. What clarifications were made to help distinguish the group for Christian readers?
   c. See if you can find out where the name came from and when it was created.
   d. Write convincing definitions as might be written by (1) an angry atheist and (2) a divisive Christian in another denomination.
7. Repeat Question 6 with the term *fundamentalism*.
8. Read *How to Lie with Statistics* by Darryl Huff. This is a short paperback written for the common man to warn him

about ways that people manipulate numbers in order to deceive or mislead.

    a. Explain ways that each of the following words can misrepresent facts, according to Huff (chapter references are for his book mentioned above).

        1) average (Ch. 2 and 3)

        2) twice, double, triple (Ch. 6)

        3) more (Ch. 8)

        4) causes (Ch. 8)

        5) percentage (Ch. 9)

    b. What are Huff's five steps for avoiding being misled (Ch. 10)?

    c. Find an editorial or advertisement that plays on an emotionally charged word to convince people of something.

9. Define *logic*. You may use a dictionary.

10. The most famous logicians of the 1900s were Alfred North Whitehead and Bertrand Russell. Write a paragraph about them. Include the dates during which they lived, the main book that they collaborated on, and their philosophical goal(s).

Methods of Definition

Now that you see the importance of definitions, how can you improve your use of them? This chapter presents four methods of definition to aid your selection of the best technique for each situation. Guidelines for properly employing each technique will also be given.

Concepts

The four methods of definition are classification, synonym, example, and development.

Definition by Classification—**Classification** is the most important method of definition. In biology, animals are classified by determining their family and species. The family name gives the broad category or context. The species distinguishes each animal from others in the same family. This provides a very precise method of classification. The same method can be used to define other words. For example, a *utensil* is a tool for domestic work, while an *instrument* is a tool for precision work. In both definitions *tool* is the broad group or family. In each case the term is distinguished from other tools by specifying the type of work for which it is used. This is the clearest and most precise method, but care is needed because two claims are made in a single statement: (1) a utensil is a tool, and (2) utensils are used domestically.

Definitions of the classification type are always reversible. This means that you can also draw a third conclusion: a tool that is also used domestically is a *utensil*. This conclusion reverses the order of the original definition. Definitions contain a lot of information, so be careful when you write or apply definitions.

Definition by Synonym—The **synonym** method defines a term by comparing it to another simpler word. This method is the easiest, but it is less precise than classification. If the word *utensil* is defined as a "tool," the distinguishing connotations are lost. You would not usually speak of hoes as farm utensils or swords as military utensils, but they are both tools. Still, the basic idea of *utensils* has been communicated. This suggests that this method of definition is appropriate in casual communication or general discussion in which precision is not expected or where brevity is appreciated. Another disadvantage of this method is that such informal definitions are not reversible. Finally, it is also difficult to define the basic term *tool* without using *utensil*. This would make the definitions circular. Fortunately, it is rare when you need to define the broader, more basic term.

Definition by Example—The **example** method defines a term by pointing to instances of the term or by listing representative elements or types of the term. *Utensil* could be defined by pointing to a pan as an example. The disadvantage here is that the concept *pan* might be interpreted as the meaning of *utensil*. On the other hand, this is the primary way to define terms for small children. In fact, we all learned the word *dog* this way. Definition by example offers the most readily understandable method. Everyone appreciates examples because they are easy to relate to. Examples bring terms down to a very practical level. Since examples are so important to communication, you must seek to reduce chances of misinterpretation. One way to avoid this is to give several examples, not just one. If the examples are representative and not all the same, the general class is more easily discerned. Showing a child ten different-sized pans may help his concept of *pan*, but it will not help his definition of *utensil*. But imagine the four examples: fork, pan, ladle, and pot. These four examples are better than ten pans because the representative sample of utensils guides you toward the correct generalization. Definitions by example are not reversible, but the correct generalization is reversible.

This method can be lengthy. The correct "mammal" concept would require long lists of examples to define this way. If your list did not include whales, bats, kangaroos, and platypuses, many wrong concepts of mammals could result. This method, therefore, is best employed as a communication aid or as a supplement to a more precise method of definition.

Definition by Development—The **development** method defines a term by applying the derivation or root meaning of a word together with the historical changes in its usage. The word's origin and development is thereby summarized. Both derivation and history can be helpful, but neither infallibly determines meaning. Development definitions must be used cautiously.

The word *astronomy* derives from two Latin words that literally mean "law of the stars" (*aster* = star, *nomos* = law). This derivation can help you remember the meaning of the word, which is the science of the stars. It can also expand your vocabulary. When you see the word *astrophysics*, you know it has to do with stars (aster). You can also identify words like *gastronomy* and *agronomy* as sciences (nomos). If one includes the history of the word's usages, a long stride toward characterizing the word will have been achieved.

You can see that derivations can help you to remember words, expand vocabulary, and identify possible meanings of a word. The derivation provides excellent background material, but be aware of its limitations. *Astrology* has a derivation similar to *astronomy* and literally means "study of the stars" (*aster* = star, *ology* = study). However, astrology does not refer to a scientific study of stars; rather it refers to occult practices relating to the stars (be sure you know the difference between "cult" and "occult"). *Astrology* is a study of stars for the purpose of fortunetelling. This clearly distinguishes it from astronomy. Fortunetelling is harmful, and God forbids its practice. Thus, the derivation can be very misleading.

Applications

History—Suppose that you are assigned to write a paper on a revolution. You are given the choice of writing on a political revolution in a Third World nation or a philosophical revolution in a major Western nation. Your choice of topic will influence your definition of the key term *revolution,* and your definition may guide your entire paper!

If you choose to write your paper on a philosophical revolution, your main point may be that it really was a revolution. This can be argued only by showing that the results fit the definition of a revolution. Each conclusion from the definition will have to be addressed, and these points may serve as the major points (Roman numerals) in your outline and determine the paragraphs in your paper. Use a neutral source (dictionary) for your definition and explain the definition clearly with synonyms and examples. If your definition is not understood, the reason for your points and outline will be clouded.

If you choose a revolution in a small country, it may be clear that it was a revolution. You may need to show what lessons can be drawn from it. Here too, though, it will be more difficult to explain the lessons of the revolution if you do not see clearly why it is a revolution. If *revolution* refers mainly to rebellions, the lesson will be different than if it refers to replacements. Your lesson will be understood by your reader more clearly if you take the time to define your main term. In fact, if you choose an unsuccessful revolution, you still may need to argue that it really was a revolution as previously discussed.

The definition should not be circular, foggy, too broad, or too narrow. Consider the following definitions of *revolution*. Notice how the various definitions influence the entire paper.

1. *Revolution* means social pressure from revolutionaries.

2. *Revolution* means upstart punks who pillage.

3. *Revolution* means successive attempts to govern.

4. *Revolution* means a replacement of an established government with a new one.

5. *Revolution* means an attempted overthrow of an established government from within.

The first definition is circular. The term *revolutionaries* depends on the root concept of a revolution for meaning. A revolutionary is defined as one who participates in or organizes a revolution. This approach is simply using the basic term to define a related term. Related terms will be understood as long as the basic term *revolution* is clearly defined without using the related terms. Take this precaution to avoid circular definitions.

The second definition is foggy because of poor grammar and emotionally laden words. A revolution is not a person; it is an event. The writer probably means "pillaging by punks." The grammatical error clouds the meaning; the emotional words also cloud the meaning. Was the American Revolution that won our freedom begun by "pillaging punks?" Also, it is hard to prove that a group of people are punks. Even if proof of looting is presented, the paper will not be conclusive. What makes a thief a punk? Using correct grammar and avoiding those emotional words will clear up the fog and strengthen the conclusions.

The third definition is also foggy. This time the confusion concerns the word *successive*. The phrase makes sense grammatically but can be taken in different ways. Perhaps the student just meant that one government replaces (or succeeds) the previous one. Alternately, he may have meant "a serious, determined attempt to take over" (successive attempts showing the determination of the revolutionaries). A casual reader may even think the student confused "successive" with "successful." If so, perhaps he meant "a successful overthrow of a government."

Any of these three possibilities could be made clear by rewording. Examples could also be used for clarification. Notice that in each case the student will be attempting to show something different in the paper. The paper is certain to receive a low grade if the teacher cannot decipher what the student is trying to show. The most convincing arguments of "serious repeated attempts" are empty if the reader thinks the goal is to show that the "revolutionaries made a successful overthrow." Examples and proper word choice can help to remove this fog.

The fourth and fifth definitions illustrate the problem of scope. The fourth is too broad since it would include any military takeover. Was Iraq's takeover of Kuwait a revolution? It did attempt to replace the government! The fifth definition, while not too broad, is probably too narrow. No paper could show that the Industrial Revolution was an attempt to overthrow the government. For a philosophical revolution, the scope would have to be broadened to include "restructuring of established systems."

As noted above, examples can be given to clarify, but any examples given should also be clear, not obscure. A student who uses definition four, even though it is broad, may write a successful paper if his examples make his meaning clearer: "Examples of revolutions that replaced governments include the American Revolution (1775), the French Revolution (1789), and the Russian Revolution (1917)." Each of these examples is well known. The reader knows that the established government was replaced in each case. This clarifies the intended meaning of the definition. In fact, since the American Revolution did not replace the entire British government, but only the government of one region under its jurisdiction, the writer clearly intends this situation to be classified under his definition also. The writer has removed the fog from the reader's mind by well-chosen examples.

On the other hand, he could write "Some examples are the revolutions of Peron, the Sandinistas, and the 1848 June Days." If the reader is not familiar with any of these, the writer has not clarified his meaning. If the reader is familiar with any of them, the meaning is still not clear. Why was Peron chosen? Peron became president in Argentina, but this was long after his revolutionary activities. He held political office before he took the presidency. Furthermore, he was later exiled to Spain. It is not clear whether he participated in an overthrow or whether an attempted overthrow was successful. Thus the example does not illustrate either possible meaning, and it actually creates more confusion.

You have seen then that the fifth definition (or the fourth, if explained with clear and familiar examples) will properly guide the main points. The writer must show three things: first, that there was an established government, second, that there was an attempt to overthrow or take over that government, and third, that the group of people who made the attempt were citizens of the country. If these three points are made clearly, the paper will be a success. You also learned that to write a successful paper on a philosophical revolution, such as the Industrial Revolution, you will need to modify your definition of *revolution* to "a restructuring of an established system." This definition will require three main points. First, describe the established system. Second, show that the changes were comprehensive enough to be called a restructuring of society. Third, demonstrate that these changes could be traced to the same internal cause. Notice that these are the conclusions implied by the definition. Since the definition is reversible, if you show these three things about your subject (the Industrial Revolution), you have shown that it is an instance covered by your term (philosophical revolution). Are you surprised at how much the definition influences your communication (and grade)?

Bible—Understanding the words of the Bible takes careful study. The word *conversation* will illustrate the importance of derivational word study. Since the writing of the King James Version (KJV) nearly 400 years ago, many words have changed meaning. The word *conversation* is one of these words. A dictionary from King James's time would give the synonym "conduct." Hebrews 13:5 says "Let your conversation be without covetousness." Today you might think that this is a command to watch your speech and that you should not talk about getting more possessions.

However, when you read it for what it meant when it was written, you see that it was a much stronger command. In fact, your thoughts, as well as your speech should be without greed. You must be content in life. This principle is reinforced by the rest of the verse. Most of the time that the word *conversation* appears in the KJV, it means conduct. This illustrates how English words develop in meaning. For English literature of the past, like Shakespearean literature, a modern dictionary is helpful but not always conclusive. Care must be taken to find Shakespeare's intended meaning using the word meanings of his day.

Furthermore, the Bible is a translation of an ancient book. For books not originally written in English, even an old English dictionary may not help. Since the Bible was written in Greek, Hebrew, and Aramaic, it is the meanings of the words in these languages that are the final authority. This is one reason that a pastor's knowledge of these languages is especially helpful to English-speaking Christians. For instance, the word *conversation* occurs again in Philippians 3:20. But in this passage it does not mean "speech" (modern English) or "conduct" (early English); instead, it translates a different Greek word meaning "citizenship." This verse is one of the few instances in the Bible that mention our heavenly citizenship. This verse is a wonderful promise, but you lose the blessing if you miss the intended meaning of the word *conversation.*

Remember to interpret a word based on (1) the meaning it had at the time of writing, (2) the word in the original language, and (3) the context. Do not force derivations or history into the author's word choice!

You can see why Paul admonished Timothy to "study to shew thyself approved unto God" (II Tim. 2:15) and why the Jews who understood only the Babylonian language after their captivity needed special help from the scribes to understand the Hebrew Scriptures: "So they read in the book in the law of God distinctly, and gave the sense, and *caused them to understand* the reading" (Neh. 8:8).

Memory Verse—Hebrews 11:1
   "Now faith is the substance of things hoped for, the evidence
   of things not seen."

In this verse there is a definition by classification. The word family to which faith belongs is "substance"; the idea here is the state of assurance or being sure. The type of "substance" is "of things hoped for." This distinguishes faith from other kinds of assurance or confidence—such as confidence in riches as exemplified by the rich man in Luke 12:16-21. The very next phrase "the evidence of things not seen" confirms this interpretation. "Evidence" also means conviction or certainty. "Things not seen" distinguishes hope from visible wealth or power. This verse reminds you that classification definitions imply several conclusions. First, faith is assurance or certainty; second, faith is not a trust in riches or power but in things invisible and hoped for. The passage goes on to give examples of right faith: Abraham hoped for the city of God (Heb. 11: 9-16). Some people hope for nothingness when they die. The reversible definition in the memory verse classifies confident hope for nothingness as faith, but the examples in the subsequent verses show that such faith is not a right faith.

Classification is not the only method of definition used in Scripture. The example method is used in Luke 10:25-37 (see Question 2).

The synonym method is also used in the Bible. The Bible defines sin in I John 3:4, which states "Whosoever committeth sin transgresseth also the law: for sin is the transgression of the law." The phrase "transgression of the law" is a translation of a single Greek word which literally means "lawlessness." You can see that "sin is lawlessness" defines sin using the synonym "lawlessness."

Conclusion

Four methods of definition have been presented: classification, synonym, example, and development. Each has advantages and disadvantages. Each is useful in its place, but each method will be more effective if certain guidelines are followed.

The first three types (characterization, synonym, and example) were relevant for writing the history paper on a "revolution." The last type (development) helped you understand the term "conversation" in the Bible.

The Bible actually illustrates all four methods of definition and provides a good model for appropriate uses of all four. The Bible uses definitions by characterization in Hebrews 11:1, by example in Luke 10:25-37, or by synonym in I John 3:4. Definition by development is demonstrated by Hebrews 13:5 or Nehemiah 8:8.

Method	(A)dvantages (D)isadvantages	Appropriate Uses	Guidelines
Classification	**(A)** precise reversible **(D)** least familiar two implications	(1) specialized terms (2) key words in essays (3) dictionaries (4) always helpful when explained	(1) Avoid circularity. (2) Clarify, eliminate fog— avoid poor grammar and emotional words. (3) Set scope—not too broad or too narrow.
Synonym	**(A)** brevity **(D)** imprecise	(1) general discussion (2) casual talk (3) supplement other methods	(1) Avoid circularity—not for basic vocabulary. (2) Seek word with closest connotation.
Example	**(A)** accessible **(D)** imprecise	(1) with children (2) basic vocabulary (3) supplement other methods	(1) Explain how it is an example. (2) Give many examples. (3) Use representative examples. (4) Use familiar examples.
Development	**(A)** memory aid vocabulary builder background material **(D)** may not apply	(1) derivations that help to show meaning (2) historical usages for literature (3) translated works	(1) Use only in context. (2) Emphasize meaning at time of writing. (3) Emphasize meaning in original language.

Terms

classification

development

example

synonym

Questions

1. The following lists of examples define *island*. Choose the best one and identify the weaknesses of the others.

    a. Long Island, Oahu, Cuba, Mackinac Island

    b. Oahu, Philippines, Madagascar, Staten Island

    c. Komodo, Honshu, Mauritius, Niihau

    d. Staten Island, Long Island, Easter Island, Isle of Wight

    e. Manhattan, Borneo, Iceland, Cuba

    f. Kodiak Island, New Guinea, Iceland, Cuba

2. Look up each passage and explain what word is being defined by example.

    a. Luke 10:25-37

    b. Matthew 5:21-26

3. Which are definitions? For each definition determine which method was used.

    a. *Meekness* means power under control.

    b. *Computers* are machines.

    c. *Machines* are computers.

    d. *Polygon* means many angles (*poly* = many + *gonu* = knee).

    e. *Insolence* is rebellion.

    f. *Quick* formerly meant ''alive.''

    g. *Pets* are fun.

4. Decide whether the definition is too broad or too narrow (or both). Give an example to justify your conclusion; then correct the definition.

    a. *Narwhal* refers to a mammal with a horn.

    b. *Birds* are flying creatures.

    c. *Verbs* are words of action.

    d. *Fainted* means ''collapsed.''

5. *Grace* has been defined as ''unmerited favor.'' Identify its word family and type. State two implications of the definition. Give an example of something in the family but not the type.

6. Why is it improper to define a *procedure* as an ''algorithm''?

7. Evaluate your definition of *logic* from Chapter 1, Question 9. Write a definition by classification that improves your previous definition.

8. Chapter 1 of *Exegetical Fallacies* by D. A. Carson (pp. 25-66) discusses word study fallacies. He presents several types of mistakes made in Bible interpretation because of misunderstanding or misusing definitions of words. Though the chapter is not light reading, you can grasp the main ideas of his discussion. Read and summarize the problem he discusses in each section below:

   a. pp. 26-32

   b. pp. 32-34

   c. pp. 34-36

   d. pp. 41-43

9. Play a few games of Balderdash or Bible Balderdash and use the guidelines in forming your definitions. Notice that your definitions will be selected more frequently when they follow those rules.

10. Write a paragraph about Kurt Gödel (sometimes spelled Goedel). Include principal dates, place of birth, teaching career, famous theorem, and how the theorem refuted Russell and Whitehead.

Statements and Truth Values

Which sentences are statements? What makes a statement true or false, and how can one know? This chapter addresses these questions. You constantly evaluate the truth of statements. News broadcasts and commercials are always making claims, and much of what is said is debatable. Some of these claims are mere predictions; yet others are totally false. You also need to carefully evaluate legal statements as well as claims concerning Scripture. This chapter introduces tips and tools to help you evaluate effectively.

Concepts

Five sentence types—A statement is a sentence that is true or false. Not every sentence is true or false. Can you evaluate the following sentences as true or false?

1. Good morning, Penny!
2. Why are you in a hurry?
3. Please, let it rain.
4. Bring your coat, Robert!

It is useless to assign **truth value** (true or false) to these sentences. There are five types of sentences: exclamations, questions, requests, commands, and statements. The sentences listed above are examples of the four types of sentences that are not statements. The most difficult of these types to identify is the request. **Requests** include both wishes (general requests) and prayers (requests to God). Requests are distinguished from **questions** by the lack of a question mark. Requests differ from **commands** in that either an imperative is lacking or the sentence is softened. Requests also differ from **exclamations**. Exclamations are spontaneous expressions of surprise, fear, or even thanksgiving, whereas, with a request, the speaker is seeking something. The fifth type of sentence is the statement. A **statement** is a sentence that is true or false from God's perspective.

Truth values—Consider the following sentences that are statements:

1. George Washington was the first president of the United States.
2. Brazil is a Swedish colony.
3. Vega appears brighter than any other star in the constellation Lyra.
4. The universe is infinite.

The first is a true statement; the second is a false statement. You can classify these two statements easily. The third is true, but you may need to consult a reference book to know for sure. The fourth, however, cannot be decided conclusively this side of heaven. You may be able to collect limited evidence for one view or the other, but no living person can prove conclusively that it is true or false. On the other hand, God certainly knows what He created. God could easily classify it as true or false. The sentence is a statement since it is true or false from God's perspective. Consequently, you can classify all four sentences as statements, even though in this life you may never know the truth value of the fourth.

It is a common error to confuse form with meaning. Read Romans 6:2—"How shall we, that are dead to sin, live any longer therein?" This is a question and is neither true nor false. On the other hand, in the context of Romans it is a rhetorical question, and the expected answer is "we should not." This means that the question is being used to suggest the true statement: Those who are dead to sin should not live any longer in sin. It is important to distinguish the question (which is not even a statement) from the true statement that the rhetorical question implies. Without this distinction, you will constantly confuse form (question or statement) with meaning (true or false). It is incorrect to say that the question is true, but you can say that the implied statement is true.

Negating—The **negation** of a statement is a statement that has the opposite truth value of the original statement. If the original statement is true, the negation must be false. If a statement is false, its negation must be true. Thus, it must be impossible for a statement and its negation to be both true or both false at the same time. These facts can be summarized by a chart called a **truth table.**

In the chart below, S represents the original statement. Since the symbol "~" represents negation, ~S represents the negation of statement S. The first row shows that when S is true, the negation is false. What does the second row mean?

S	~S
T	F
F	T

Do not confuse negations with opposites. You usually think of black and white as opposites. Are the following statements negations of each other?

1. This bear is white.
2. This bear is black.

If both statements can be true at the same time or false at the same time, they are not negations. A bear that is not a white polar bear is not necessarily black; it may be brown. Since both can be false at the same time, they are not negations. Remember, the negation of something must take a position that is true whenever the original is false. Do not think of opposites. A person who wants to argue the point does not have to say the bear is black; any color bear that is not white will do. The negation must be "this bear is not white."

Think about the statement "Joe is unconcerned." The negation is "Joe is not unconcerned," but in this case "not unconcerned" does mean "concerned." Since it is clearer to use a positive statement rather than a double negative when possible, "Joe is concerned" is the best negation. In this case, negation is indicated by using a word other than "not."

In the first example, you found the negation of the positive statement "This bear is white." The next example began with a negative statement: "Joe is unconcerned." A negatively phrased statement is still a statement. Notice that it was the S in the chart, and "Joe is concerned" was the ~S. What if you started with "Joe is concerned" and negated it twice? The first negation is "Joe is unconcerned," and the next is back to the original "Joe is concerned.''After two negations, you will always get back to the original. The truth table proves this:

S	~S	~(~S)
T	F	T
F	T	F

The ~S column is filled in by switching the truth values for S. Then ~(~S) is figured by reversing the truth values for ~S. Since the S and ~(~S) values are the same, the chart proves that two negations get back to the original. This is the **double negation rule** which is stated as follows:

$$\sim(\sim S) = S$$

Categoricals—A **categorical statement** is a statement that classifies (or categorizes) objects. The following statements using x and y show the four types of categoricals. You can describe the **quality** of a categorical statement as **positive** or **negative.** You can immediately see which two are negative and which two are positive.

All x are y.
Some x are not y.
Some x are y.
No x are y.

Besides classifying quality, you can also classify the **quantity** of categoricals. The quantity of a categorical is either universal or particular. The statements with ''all'' and ''no'' are **universal,** and those with ''some'' are **particular.** The universal statements are not negations of each other. Just because the statement ''All engineers are geniuses'' is false does not mean that none are geniuses. If you know one engineer that is not a genius, you know that ''All engineers are geniuses'' is false, but saying ''No engineers are geniuses'' is much too strong; maybe there is one working at another company! To negate ''all x are y,'' write ''at least one x is not a y.'' The phrase ''at least one'' is the meaning of the word ''some,'' so ''some x are not y'' is the proper negation. Likewise, the negation for ''no x are y'' must be that ''at least one x is y,'' or more simply ''some x are y.'' Similarly, the particular statements are not negations of each other.

Be careful of negating categorical statements. Just inserting "not" will not create the proper negation. Think about how you would challenge or argue the point.

Applications

Law—Think of a state that uses the death penalty for a person convicted of murder. Imagine that the law reads this way: "All murder is punishable with death." A lawyer must be careful as he constructs his case. Suppose that he is prosecuting a man who has confessed murder. Notice the mistake if he takes this approach: "the man must receive the death penalty by law because otherwise the law is nullified or disproved." This lawyer claims that the law and an unpunished murderer cannot both be true. He is arguing that an unpunished murderer is contrary to or is a negation of the law statement. Is he right? Look again:

Statement: All murder is punishable with death.
Negation: Some murder is not punishable with death.

The negation does not say "Some murder is not punished with death." Punished and punishable are not the same. The unpunished murderer was not punished, but he could have been. The lawyer has not shown that this law is violated. The murderer was punishable, but not punished. On the other hand, there may be many other good arguments for punishment. The lawyer could have made a stronger case for punishment by arguing that the unpunished murderer sets a precedent contrary to the intent of the law, but the case presented instead is weak. He saw a contradiction where there was none. This example reinforces the importance of words (punished or punishable), but it also illustrates the importance of correctly negating statements. To argue a point, the truth value of the statements and the opposing position (negation statement) must be clearly in view. Here you switch from emphasis on the meanings of individual words to the meanings of combinations of words.

As another example in the area of criminal law, imagine that Jim is a shoe store salesman. The store prosecutes him for embezzling money. Suppose Jim convinces the court that the store's clerk kept inaccurate records. Jim claims innocence, indicating that the clerk is at fault. Notice how the claim diverts suspicion without proving Jim's innocence. Perhaps the clerk was an accomplice, but suppose that Jim proves they were not working together. The clerk's inaccuracy means "Some of the financial imbalances are due to the clerk" (and not Jim). The statement of Jim's guilt is "some financial imbalance is due to Jim" (not the clerk). These two statements are not negations. They could both be true at once. The truth of one does not prove the falsity of the other. To show the guilt statement false, he would have to prove that "All the financial imbalances are due to the clerk" (and not Jim). Lawyers must carefully evaluate the truth of statements and also the relation between statements and negations.

News—Fallacies will be discussed in Chapters 9 and 10. However, a warning will be helpful here. Imagine that Troy, a humanist, writes an editorial on the lack of professionalism in a local Christian elementary school.

Now every Christian will disagree with humanism, and perhaps you think that Troy is wrong about the school also. If you decide to write a letter to the editor, be careful. Decide which issue you will address and stick to it.

If you want to defend the school, the negation of Troy's statement is "the local Christian school is professional." You cannot support your position by criticizing Troy or his philosophy of humanism. Even if you prove to everyone that humanism is wrong, you have not shown that the Christian school is professional. The error of humanism is not the negation for lack of professionalism. It could be that humanism is wrong and the school is a substandard Christian school too. In order to defend the school, you must show errors in Troy's *evidence* or provide counter evidence. This example shows that properly negating a statement is important, but negating the proper statement is more important.

Suppose Tom, a third party, responds to your letter to the editor and agrees with Troy that the school is unprofessional. Do you reply again and angrily call Tom a humanist? Again, his humanism does not follow from his position on the school issue. As another example, if you agree with a humanist that $2 + 2 = 4$, does that make you a humanist?

Furthermore, suppose you decide to write against humanism. Do not bring up the school issue at all. It is irrelevant to the philosophical position. Also, getting him to agree with part of the Bible, such as the golden rule, does not demolish his position. A person who says the Bible is not true does not mean that every word is false. His believing the golden rule does not mean he believes the whole Bible. Neither is the golden rule necessarily contradictory to any of humanism's tenets. Making such errors in writing hurts your Christian testimony to Troy and to every other reader of your letter.

Editorials and especially letters to the editor are full of such errors, but a Christian must "prove all things; hold fast that which is good" (I Thess. 5:21). Avoid making the same mistakes!

Bible—The Bible contains all five types of sentences discussed earlier. Examples of each are given below.

1. Exclamations: "Amen." (Rev. 22:21) "Father, I thank thee that thou hast heard me." (John 11:41)
2. Questions: "Where have ye laid him?" (John 11:34)
3. Requests: "The grace of our Lord Jesus Christ be with you all." (Rev. 22:21)
4. Commands: "Lazarus, come forth." (John 11:43)
5. Statements: "He that seeth me seeth him that sent me." (John 12:45)

There are many statements in Scripture. They are phrased both negatively and positively. It is often (but not always) simplest to represent negatively phrased statements as negations of a positive statement. John 12:47 contains a negatively phrased statement: "I came not to judge the world." The statement in John 11:23 "Thy brother shall rise again" is positively phrased. Either statement could be represented by S. However, either could also be represented as $\sim S$. John 12:47 is $\sim S$ if S is "I came to judge the world." This is natural since the $\sim$ reflects the word "not" in John 12:47. John 11:23 is $\sim S$ if S is "thy brother shall not rise again." This is not natural but may occasionally be useful.

So far all of the statements have been true. The Bible also reports false statements, especially when it quotes evil beings such as Satan in Isaiah 14:14: "I will be like the most High." Verse 15 makes the falsehood clear. God asserts that Satan will not be like God, but rather will be brought down to hell. Notice that this quote from the devil is contained in a sentence beginning in verse 13, "For thou hast said in thine heart. " This sentence is true, because Satan did think those evil thoughts.

The difference between a false statement and the true report of the false statement is important. Verses can be found like Isaiah 14:14

which are false in themselves, and others, like Revelation 22:21, are neither true nor false, since they are not statements. Yet still, when the verses are examined in context, no sentence in the Bible can be said to be false. "The Bible is true" is not a dishonest statement.

In addition, all four types of categoricals appear in Scripture.

Particular Positive: "Some [people] are puffed up." (I Corinthians 4:18)

Particular Negative: "Some believed not." (Acts 28:24) (Or paraphrased as a categorical statement, "some people are not believers.")

Universal Positive: "All have sinned." (Romans 3:23) (All men are sinners.)

Universal Negative: "No man hath seen God."(John 1:18) (No man is a person who sees God.)

Notice that Romans 3:23 is a statement stressing that everyone has done evil. You usually consider evil to be negative, but do not use value judgments in classifying categorical statements. The negative idea of evil does not make the statement negative. Classifications must be based on word choice. Since the sentence does not use the words "not," "no," "none," or negative prefixes like "un-," the statement is positive. The same thought may be expressed negatively: "No man has done good." How a statement is expressed can be as important as the thought expressed.

Memory Verse—John 17:17

"Sanctify them through thy truth: thy word is truth."

John 17 is part of Jesus' prayer to God for His disciples. The first part of the memory verse is Jesus' request. It is not a statement. It could be a command, but this book classifies desires expressed in prayers as requests. The second part of the verse is a statement. The statement is true and positively phrased. It affirms that the Bible is true. You have already seen that this is reasonable.

The previous discussions indicate that Jesus does not mean that nothing false appears in biblical phrases. But He does mean that reports of false statements are true in that they are accurately reported. No teaching of Scripture is false. No reference to historical or scientific information is false or inaccurate. Likewise, when taken in context, no proper implication of a question, command, request, or exclamation is false.

The Bible is the one document that can be relied upon if the reader will understand its statements in context and seek the help of the Holy Spirit in understanding God's intended meaning.

Conclusion

You studied five types of sentences: exclamation, question, request, command, and statement. The last type is either true or false. You noted that statements can be positively or negatively phrased. The negation of the statement has the opposite truth value of the original. Truth tables clarify negations. This symbolic tool will also provide insight into other concepts. Besides being positive or negative, categorical statements are either universal or particular. Universal statements make all-inclusive claims (all or none), and particular statements make only individual claims (some).

CATEGORICAL STATEMENTS

		Quantity	
		Universal	Particular
Quality	Positive	All A are B.	Some A are B.
	Negative	No A are B.	Some A are not B.

The arrows above show which statements are negations of each other.

All of these types of sentences appear in the Scriptures and in legal contexts. Remember that every statement of Scripture in context is true (John 17:17).

Terms

categorical statement

commands

double negation rule

exclamations

negation

negative

particular

positive

quality (of a categorical statement)
quantity (of a categorical statement)
questions
requests
statements
truth table
truth value
universal

Questions

1. Identify the type of sentence found in each Bible reference.

    a. II Corinthians 9:15

    b. I Thessalonians 5:17

    c. I Thessalonians 5:9

    d. I Thessalonians 2:19a

    e. I Thessalonians 5:23

2. Identify the following types of sentences.

    a. Vanity of vanities!

    b. Mom, buy me a candy bar.

    c. Mom, may I have a candy bar, please?

    d. Mom, it sure would be great to have a candy bar.

    e. Mom, Joey gets millions of candy bars every day.

3. For each categorical statement, mark it *true* or *false* and give its negation. If it is *false,* give an example as proof.

    a. All birds can fly.

    b. Some mammals fly.

    c. No mammal lays eggs.

    d. Some vegetables are not green.

4. Mark each statement *true* or *false.*

    a. "Yet will I not deny thee." (Matt. 26:35)

    b. "The waters prevailed upon the earth an hundred and fifty days." (Gen. 7:24)

    c. The sun is the only star that appears brighter than Sirius.

    d. Istanbul is the capital of Turkey.

e. Richard, earl of Cornwall, was not a king of England from the house of York.

f. James K. Polk was the tenth president of the United States.

g. The negation of a universal categorical is a particular categorical.

5. Negate each statement in Question 4.

6. For each false statement in Question 4, give an example which shows that the negation is true.

7. Read John 11:47-52. What did Caiaphas, the Pharisees, and the chief priests want to do? Was it evil? Did Caiaphas speak the truth (in verse 50) according to the following verses?

8. Matilda wanted an abortion. Matilda was refused, and she died in childbirth. Does this prove that abortion should be permitted? Why or why not?

9. Think about a light switch that controls the electricity to a light. How could negations be used to represent the electricity?

10. Write a paragraph on Chrysippus. For content, include the years of his birth and death, his birthplace, and his contributions to logic. How do his contributions relate to this chapter on statements and truth values?

CHAPTER 4
Connectives and Truth Values

The previous chapter discussed sentence types. Throughout the rest of the book, you will focus on only one of the types: statements. Truth or falsity applies to every statement, but to this point in the discussion you have considered simple statements only. Perhaps some of them did not seem simple, but "simple" refers to a statement with no connectives. Notice that sentences like the ones below have not been previously discussed:

"God created the world, or it evolved by itself."
"Some men are murderers, but some men are not."
"If you eat your spinach, you may have ice cream."
"Those rules apply only on alternate Thursdays."

In this chapter you will learn about the connectives in these sentences and how to determine their truth values. One of the most valuable tools for studying such statements is the truth table.

Concepts
Unconditional Connectives—The two most common connectives are AND and OR. Suppose you tell me, "I saw John and Mary at the store." This compound means both "I saw John at the store" and "I saw Mary at the store." If in actuality you did not see John, then you have lied even if you did see Mary. What if someone says, "I love Jane, but Jane loves Dave." For the statement to be true, both parts must be true. Notice that the word *but* means the same as *and;* however, it gives a connotation of contrast. Several words mean the same as *and* including *yet, both,* and *also.* Even semicolons are used in this way. Replace *but* with a semicolon to see for yourself. The two-part claim, called a **conjunction,** is the most

common sentence using a connective. The symbol ∧ will be used to represent the concept AND. Remember that a conjunction is a compound statement that is true only if both parts are true. The word *and* is the usual signal for conjunctions, but other words, as mentioned earlier, can be used too. Using P = "I saw John" and Q = "I saw Mary," then $P ∧ Q$ represents the original statement "I saw John and Mary."

"Either Pete or Penny will win the contest." Now, if the winner is Clara, then the statement above is false. It is true as long as at least one of the two parts (Pete won, Mary won) is true. If Pete won and not Penny, if Penny won and not Pete, or even if they tied and both won, no one can accuse the speaker of lying. This means that OR statements are true if either part is true. Such a statement is called a **disjunction** and is symbolized by ∨ to represent the concept OR. Using the letters P = "Pete will win" and Q = "Penny will win," then $P ∨ Q$ represents the original compound statement.

To represent these compounds with **truth tables,** both parts (P and Q) must be represented. Notice that there are four possibilities: (1) both true, (2) P true, Q false, (3) P false, Q true, and (4) both false. You should always list the four possibilities in that order. Notice that True and False alternate in pairs in the first column (P) and individually in the second column (Q). Fill in the third column according to the correct answer for each row. For instance, the second row of the $P ∧ Q$ table must be filled in as False because when P is True and Q is False, the conjunction P and Q is False.

Conjunction				Disjunction		
P	Q	$P∧Q$		P	Q	$P∨Q$
T	T	T		T	T	T
T	F	F		T	F	T
F	T	F		F	T	T
F	F	F		F	F	F

These charts conveniently summarize the discussion. Notice that there is only one T in the conjunction column (∧) and the rest are Fs. Remembering this true case will help you remember the whole chart. In contrast, the disjunction (∨) column has only one F, and the rest are Ts. This false case will help you remember the chart. In summary: AND (∧) is true only when both parts are true, but OR (∨) is always true unless both parts are false.

Finally, it saves a lot of writing to show the truth tables in a shorter format as follows, but be careful because the answer is in the middle column (shaded)—not at the right. You will see how much writing time these truth tables save later in this chapter.

P	$\wedge$	Q		P	$\vee$	Q
T	T	T		T	T	T
T	F	F		T	T	F
F	F	T		F	T	T
F	F	F		F	F	F

Conditional Connectives—Whenever a statement can be paraphrased using the "if P then Q" format, the statement is a **conditional statement.** A conditional statement is also called an **implication,** and its symbol is →. The arrow symbol means IMPLIES.

Consider the conditional statement, "If Fido is a dog, then Fido is a mammal." The *if* clause, "Fido is a dog," is the **condition,** P (also called the hypothesis or protasis). The *then* clause, "Fido is a mammal," is the **conclusion,** Q (also called the apodosis). The full statement represented P → Q is the implication.

To determine the **truth table** for an implication, you must determine whether P → Q is true in each of the four possible combinations: (1) P and Q both true, (2) P false, Q true, (3) P and Q both false, and (4) P true, Q false. Analyze these one at a time using the example involving Fido.

What happens when P and Q are both true? You know that dogs are mammals, so if "Fido is a dog" (P) is true, then "Fido is a mammal" (Q) is also true. Therefore, P → Q is a true conditional statement. The condition of being a dog guarantees the conclusion of being a mammal.

	P	Q	P → Q
dog	T	T	T

Now, suppose Sharisse has a pet cat named Fido and declares, "If Fido is a dog, then Fido is a mammal." In this case, P is false because Fido is a cat, but Q is still true since cats are mammals. Could you accuse Sharisse of lying? No. The if-then statement is hypothetical. It makes a claim about dogs. The statement "If Fido is a dog, then Fido is a mammal" does not make any claim at all when Fido is not a dog. When the condition is not met, the rest of the statement is not relevant. Since Sharisse has not lied in this case, her statement must be true.

	P	Q	P → Q
cat	F	T	T

Similarly, suppose Sharisse has a pet parakeet named Fido. In this case, P and Q are both false since parakeets are neither dogs nor mammals. Nevertheless, as before, Sharisse has not lied when she says "If Fido is a dog, then Fido is a mammal."

	P	Q	P → Q
parakeet	F	F	T

The only way to prove the statement false would be to find a dog that is not a mammal. If "Fido is a dog" is true, and the conclusion "Fido is a mammal" is false, then the conditional statement is false. Of course, there is no such animal.

	P	Q	P → Q
nonmammal dog	T	F	F

In a truth table, these possibilities are usually arranged in the order shown below.

P	Q	P → Q	
T	T	T	(dog)
T	F	F	(nonmammal dog)
F	T	T	(cat)
F	F	T	(parakeet)

Notice that when P is false, the implication is true regardless of the truth value of Q. Also, notice that the statement about Fido is a true implication because the situation nonmammal dog is impossible.

Consider another statement, "If Bubbles always lives in water (P), then Bubbles is a fish (Q)." The chart below summarizes the four possibilities again with an example for each.

P	Q	P → Q	
T	T	T	(shark)
T	F	F	(whale)
F	T	T	(African lungfish)
F	F	T	(dog)

You can see that the statement is false because there are creatures that always live in water that are not fish. The statement "Bubbles is a whale" and the statement "Bubbles is an octopus" are counterexamples. An example that disproves an implication is a **counterexample.** The only way to show that the conditional statement is in error is to show that "Bubbles always lives in water" is true and "Bubbles is a fish" is false. Remember that "Bubbles is a mouse" is *not* a counterexample; when the condition of always living in water is not met, no false claim is made. Also notice that it is possible for Bubbles to live in water and be a fish. The fact that it *can* be true does not make the implication true.

You can remember the truth table by noticing the only F entry. Remember that conditional statements are false only when P (the condition) is true and Q (the conclusion) is false. Here is the truth table for implication in the shorter format:

P	$\rightarrow$	Q
T	T	T
T	F	F
F	T	T
F	T	F

So far you have considered the statements "If Fido is a dog, then Fido is a mammal" and "If Fido is a mammal, then Fido is a dog." These statements are not the same. In fact, the first is true and the second is false. This means that you cannot just switch the order of P and Q anytime you choose. A conditional statement formed by switching the condition and conclusion is called the **converse** of the statement. You can see that the converse is not true just because the original is true. Sometimes, though, both the implication and its converse are true. This special type of conditional statement is called **biconditional,** which means two conditionals.

"Liquid A is an acid *if and only if* Liquid A turns litmus paper red." The phrase "if and only if" tells you that the statement is biconditional. The statement asserts two conditional statements:

> If Liquid A turns litmus paper red, then Liquid A is an acid. (*if* part)
>
> If Liquid A is an acid, then Liquid A turns litmus paper red. (*only if* part)

Since a biconditional asserts both directions, you can use the symbol ↔ (EQUALS). You should think of it as an equal sign for statements. The $P \rightarrow Q$ part is false only when P is true and Q is false, as noted before. But the $Q \rightarrow P$ part is false when Q is true and P is false. This means that $P \leftrightarrow Q$ is false in both instances in which one is false and the other is true. Both forms of the truth table summarize these facts.

P	Q	P ↔ Q	or	P	↔	Q
T	T	T		T	T	T
T	F	F		T	F	F
F	T	F		F	F	T
F	F	T		F	T	F

Equivalence—An **equivalence** is a biconditional that is always true. The previous example is actually an equivalence. All acids turn litmus red and no other liquids do. Both statements P and Q have the same truth value. This is the reason for the name equivalence. In the example using acids and litmus, the equivalence is often used as a definition. Read the definition of *acid* in a dictionary; one definition given is usually based on the litmus test. The importance of equivalence for definition suggests that $P \leftrightarrow Q$ could be interpreted as ''P means the same as Q.'' You have seen that $P \leftrightarrow Q$ means the same as $[P \rightarrow Q$ and $Q \rightarrow P]$. How can you demonstrate this in a truth table? It is at this stage that the shorter truth tables become very helpful. First, use the implication and biconditional tables to make the next three tables.

P	↔	Q		P	→	Q		Q	→	P
T	T	T		T	T	T		T	T	T
T	F	F		T	F	F		F	T	T
F	F	T		F	T	T		T	F	F
F	T	F		F	T	F		F	T	F

Notice that all columns marked Q have the Ts and Fs in the order T F T F, and all columns marked P have the Ts and Fs in the order T T F F. The bold columns are filled in according to the rules for → (IMPLIES) and ↔ (EQUALS) as labeled. Now remember that $P \leftrightarrow Q$ means the same as $(P \rightarrow Q$ and $Q \rightarrow P)$. Translate this sentence into symbols by replacing the expression "means the same as" with ↔ (EQUALS) and "and" with ∧ (AND).

$(P \leftrightarrow Q) \leftrightarrow [(P \rightarrow Q) \land (Q \rightarrow P)]$ **Biconditional rule (BR)**

Next, form the truth table for this statement. It is formed from the three tables above by adding two columns, one for ↔ (EQUALS) and one for ∧ (AND). Because of the grouping symbols, the ∧ (AND) column must be completed first.

(P	↔	Q)	↔	[(P	→	Q)	∧	(Q	→	P)]
T	**T**	T	**T**	T	**T**	T	T	T	**T**	T
T	**F**	F	**T**	T	**F**	F	F	F	**T**	T
F	**F**	T	**T**	F	**T**	T	F	T	**F**	F
F	**T**	F	**T**	F	**T**	F	T	F	**T**	F

To fill in the circled column marked ∧ (AND), compare the bold columns marked → (IMPLIES). The only time an AND statement is true is when both parts are true. Since each part in this case is an implication $[(P \rightarrow Q)$ and $(Q \rightarrow P)]$, you must use the bold columns to determine which truth values to put in the circled column. To fill in the shaded column marked ↔ (EQUALS), compare $P \leftrightarrow Q$ (T F F T) to the circled statement (T F F T). The biconditional is true when both parts have the same truth value. Since the columns are identical, fill in the shaded column with Ts.

Because the biconditional is always true, the two expressions are **equivalent** and they "mean the same." The rule is useful for it helps you understand the meaning of $P \leftrightarrow Q$. You can also substitute either expression in place of the other. This works the same as substitution in math: if $a + b = b + a$, you can replace either side of the equation with the other whenever you see an expression of that form.

You have studied four types of connectives. Look at the chart on the following page for a quick review. The keyword helps you when you read the symbol; it gives you the logical operation.

Connectives

Name	Symbol	Keyword	Other meanings
Conjunction	∧	AND	but, also, yet, both
Disjunction	∨	OR	either
Implication (or conditional statement)	→	IMPLIES	if . . . then
Biconditional	↔	EQUALS	if and only if

If the biconditional is not always true, the expressions are not equivalent. Study the truth table below. The F in the shaded column shows that $(A \vee A) \wedge B$ is not the same as $A \vee (A \wedge B)$.

[(A	∨	A)	∧	B	↔	[A	∨	(A	∧	B)]
T	T	T	T	T	T	T	T	T	T	T
T	T	T	F	F	F	T	T	T	F	F
F	F	F	F	T	T	F	F	F	F	T
F	F	F	F	F	T	F	F	F	F	F

Applications

Business—The difference between AND and OR affects two-signature checking accounts. Many businesses (and marriages too) want more than one person to be able to write and sign checks for the company. In this case they set up a checking account that says "Checks drawn on funds from Account #3157 must be signed by Jack E. Briggs or Arnie L. Watkins." In this case in accordance with OR, either signature is sufficient; both are also acceptable.
On the other hand, some businesses have special funds with huge amounts of money, and they want to protect all parties involved from temptation or suspicion. In this case, the company may set up an account in which two persons must sign each check. "Checks drawn on funds from Account #2369 must be signed by Jack E. Briggs and Arnie L. Watkins." Since these checks require both signatures (for example, the vice president's and the treasurer's), both men will know every time a check is written. This account is very different from the first example in which Jack can write checks without Arnie knowing.
 If both men are honest men, the two types of accounts will show the same history. All transactions will show clearly, but the first

type of account (OR) makes it easier—neither man ever needs to bother to get the other to sign also. However, if one man is dishonest or falls into temptation, the first type of account offers no protection. Notice that the difference between the two is only one word. What if the company intended to set up the second account, but failed to catch the typing mistake OR instead of AND? They would think they had hindered frauds, but the bank would see the word OR and honor checks signed by Arnie alone. Arnie might be embezzling for years before he was caught. This shows how important a single word can be in business and in contracts. But it especially shows how the truth value of the sentence is influenced. Arnie's check without Jack's signature would be caught if the contract read "and" because the requirement of Jack's signature and Arnie's signature is false when only Arnie has signed. Contracts often include conditional statements too. Consider this building contract: "The building of the house on Lot #43 will be completed by August 15, 1995, unless there are more than twenty days of rain between May 1 and August 15. Otherwise the builders must pay a $500 penalty to the buyer for each day the building remains incomplete."

Here there are multiple conditions. A quick paraphrase is "If [not done on time AND not too much rain], then pay penalty." According to AND, either condition not met (i.e., done on time or too much rain) will avoid the penalty. In which situations would you go to court for breach of contract? (Use the following codes: D = done on time, R = too much rain, and P = paid. Remember that $\sim$ means NOT.)

1.	$D,$	$R,$	P	5.	$D,$	$R,$	$\sim P$
2.	$\sim D,$	$R,$	P	6.	$\sim D,$	$R,$	$\sim P$
3.	$D, \sim R,$		P	7.	$D,$	$\sim R,$	$\sim P$
4.	$\sim D, \sim R,$		P	8.	$\sim D,$	$\sim R,$	$\sim P$

In three of these eight instances, they were not required to pay and they did not pay a penalty (5, 6, and 7). In another instance (4), they were required to pay a penalty and they did, thus fulfilling the contract. In three other cases (1, 2, and 3), they were not required to pay a penalty, but they did anyway. Whatever their reasons for such strange action, no one will complain of unfair treatment. Only in one instance (8) is there cause for litigation—conditions not met and penalty not paid.

Truth tables and symbols give you a way to organize all the possibilities clearly. Such skills are very helpful in thinking through business deals and contracts. Of course, charts can be made that do not use these logic symbols. The importance of the logic symbols is that these five simple symbols can be applied to many areas without needing a whole new course on the subject. They also give you practice developing the kinds of thinking skills that are used in other business and legal matters. Finally, they focus attention on key words in the discussion: *and, or, if . . . then.*

Test-taking—In speaking, there are many words that mean the same as these special compound words.

Conjunctions include *but, yet, also, however, neither, both,* and most punctuation marks. Some of the words imply contrast, but all of them assert both statements in the compound.

Recognition of these takes practice. Until you learn to paraphrase compound statements with the five key words (NOT, AND, OR, IMPLIES, EQUALS), you will have difficulty coming to the correct conclusion on true-false items. Study the following examples.

1. Watson made the DNA model; Mendel worked with him.
2. When a person's diet lacks iron, he develops cancer.
3. The only president killed while in office was Lincoln.
4. Neither adverbs nor adjectives modify nouns.
5. Having four equal sides is a sufficient condition for a rhombus.
6. A necessary condition for presidency is to be over forty years old.

Statement 1 is a conjunction signaled by a semicolon. Paraphrase: Watson and Mendel made the DNA model. Since it says "and," it is false because Crick, not Mendel, was the second party.

Statement 2 is conditional. Replace "when" with "if" and the comma by "then." Iron deficiency results in anemia, not cancer. So the first part can be true, but the second false. This makes the conditional statement false.

In Statement 3 be careful with the phrase "the only." This statement means if the president was not Lincoln, then he was not assassinated. This is false since Kennedy offers a counterexample.

In Statement 4 the word "nor" may remind you of "or," but this is misleading. "Neither A nor B" means not A and not B. Since adjectives do modify nouns, at least one of the two is false and the conjunction is false.

The last two are both true statements. Transform them into conditional statements to see this. Since a **sufficient condition** supplies the condition (the *if* part) of an implication, Statement 5 becomes:

If a polygon has four equal sides, then it is a rhombus.

In contrast, a **necessary condition** states the conclusion (the "then" part) of an implication. Thus, Statement 6 means:

If one is president, then he is over forty years old. If a polygon has four equal sides, then it is a rhombus.

Necessary and sufficient conditions are also used to express biconditionals. The statement below is false. Do you see why?

Bearing cones is a necessary and sufficient condition for being a pine tree.

The biconditional statement is false since cones are a necessary condition for pines, but not a sufficient condition. Bearing cones as a necessary condition means that all pine trees bear cones, which is true. However, bearing cones as a sufficient condition means that all cone-bearing trees are pines. This is false since some cones come from spruce trees.

You can see that paraphrasing statements using the five key words helps in identifying the truth value of statements from biology, history, English, and math. You must understand the statement before you can hope to correctly identify whether it is true or not.

Bible—All of the compound types can be found in Scripture. This means that the proper understanding of Scripture depends on correct concepts of what these compounds mean.

Conjunction: John 15:1 "I am the true vine, *and* my Father is the husbandman."

Disjunction: Matthew 6:24 "Either he will hate the one, and love the other; *or* else he will hold to the one, and despise the other."

Implication: II Chronicles 7:14 "*If* my people, which are called by my name, shall humble themselves, and pray, and seek my face, and turn from their wicked ways; *then* will I hear from heaven, and will forgive their sin, and will heal their land."

Biconditional: I John 5:12 "He that hath the Son hath life; and he that hath not the Son of God hath not life."

The biconditional could be stated in the form "if he has the Son, then he has life *and* if he has life, then he has the Son." This emphasizes the two conditionals. In other words "He has the Son if and only if he has life." Since it is true, it is also correct to call this an equivalence.

Memory Verse—James 2:10-11

"For whosoever shall keep the whole law, and yet offend in one point, he is guilty of all. For he that said, Do not commit adultery, said also, Do not kill. Now if thou commit no adultery, yet if thou kill, thou art become a transgressor of the law."

What a great passage. You can use it to show people they are sinners since no one has kept the whole law. The passage also teaches the concept of AND presented in this chapter. The law prohibits adultery *and* murder. The passage says if the first is true, and the second false, then the whole compound is false. Conjunction (AND) is true only when both parts are true. You have not kept the law unless you keep all of its parts.

Conclusion

This chapter presented four kinds of compound statements: conjunction, disjunction, conditional, and biconditional. The truth tables given below provide insight into the meaning of each compound and prepare you for more complex applications.

A	B	Conjunction $A \wedge B$	Disjunction $A \vee B$	Conditional $A \rightarrow B$	Biconditional $A \leftrightarrow B$
T	T	T	T	T	T
T	F	F	T	F	F
F	T	F	T	T	F
F	F	F	F	T	T

Connective statements are harder than simple statements, because two statements are related in some way. Therefore, you must understand the relationship between the connected statements. The many synonyms in English for the four basic compounds make understanding even harder. The chart below summarizes the relations and meanings.

Connectives

Name	Symbol	Keyword	Other meanings
Conjunction	$\wedge$	AND	but, also, yet, both
Disjunction	$\vee$	OR	either
Implication (or conditional statement)	$\rightarrow$	IMPLIES	if . . . then
Biconditional	$\leftrightarrow$	EQUALS	if and only if

You also learned how to check for equivalent forms of expression. Truth tables provide an orderly method, but they may be lengthy. To construct a truth table do the following:

1. Set up a table with one row for each possible combination of Ts and Fs. When there are two letters in the expression, you will need four rows.

2. Complete all lettered columns. Be sure to fill in columns systematically to cover all combinations of T and F. Also, be sure to make columns with the same name identical.

3. Fill in the rows under the connectives in the order determined by grouping symbols. Use the four patterns given above and the pattern for negation that you learned in Chapter 3.

It seems as though every area uses these ideas. You found them everywhere from multiple-signature checking accounts and legal contracts to test-taking skills. The Bible has a whole lesson on *and* in James 2:10-11, the memory verse. All four connectives are found in Scripture.

The symbols and truth tables in this chapter probably seemed hard. The questions will allow you to practice with the concepts presented in this chapter. Mastery of this material provides skills for reading all kinds of subject matter and for problem solving. It also provides the main tools that will be needed in Chapters 5, 7, and 9 of this book. Yes, there are a few other difficult chapters, but the good news is that they are no harder than this one. When you master connectives and truth values, you will be encouraged. But more importantly, you should begin to use these concepts as soon as possible to improve your test-taking, reading, and interpretation skills.

Terms

biconditional

Biconditional Rule (BR)

conclusion

condition

conditional statement

conjunction

converse

counterexample

disjunction

equivalence

equivalent expressions

implication

necessary condition

sufficient condition

truth table

Questions

1. Mr. and Mrs. Stephen Kaga are a happily married Christian couple. As a couple they could obtain separate checking accounts, a joint AND checking account, or a joint OR checking account. Give an advantage of each type for the Kagas. Which will they probably want?

2. Identify similarities between separate accounts and each of the types of joint accounts.

3. Mark each sentence *true* or *false* to answer these history test items (some research may be necessary). Explain your answers.

   a. The Pure Food and Drug Act was passed during the presidency of Theodore Roosevelt and so was Prohibition.

   b. The United States neither ratified the Treaty of Versailles nor joined the League of Nations.

    c. In the Spanish-American War, Spain would not have de-
       clared war if the United States had not recognized Cuba's
       independence.

    d. The American Civil War was fought over slavery or
       states' rights.

4. Mark each sentence *true* or *false* to answer these biology test
   items (some research may be necessary). Give a counterexample for any false statement.

    a. Every plant is either a monocotyledon or a dicotyledon.

    b. If the orientation of coccus bacteria cell division is consis-
       tently in the same plane and if the daughter cells remain at-
       tached, then the resulting bacterial growth is streptococcus.

    c. If animals eat baneberries, then humans can safely eat
       baneberries also.

    d. The only predatory kind of plant is the Venus's-flytrap.

    e. All fungi are saprophytic.

    f. An organism is a plant if and only if it flowers.

    g. The term *lichen* means the same as ''a symbiosis between
       algae and a fungus.''

    h. Having gills is a necessary and sufficient condition for be-
       ing a fish.

5. Read each of the following verses in the Bible and identify
   the type of connective (if any).

    a. Romans 6:8

    b. Romans 6:23

    c. Romans 3:11a

    d. John 14:23-24

    e. Acts 7:1

    f. John 10:11

    g. Luke 11:11 (Paraphrase rhetorical questions as statements.)

6. Make a truth table for $\sim A \rightarrow \sim B$. You should realize that this
   expression means the same as the following expression with
   parentheses: $(\sim A) \rightarrow (\sim B)$.

7. Decide whether the biconditional shown is an equivalence by
   making a truth table: $(P \wedge Q) \leftrightarrow (P \rightarrow \sim Q)$

8. You have learned about the converse of an implication. Two other variations are important also. The list below summarizes important implications related to an original conditional statement.

original   If A then B ($A \rightarrow B$).

converse   If B then A ($B \rightarrow A$).

inverse   If not A then not B ($\sim A \rightarrow \sim B$).

contrapositive   If not B then not A ($\sim B \rightarrow \sim A$).

   a. Which one was repeatedly emphasized as different from the original? Check that they are not equivalent by making a truth table.

   b. Use a truth table to show that the converse and inverse are equivalent.

   c. Use a truth table to show that the contrapositive is equivalent to the original implication.

9. Match the diagrams to the compounds. (This shows how important connectives are in math.)

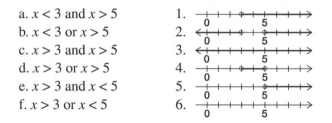

a. $x < 3$ and $x > 5$

b. $x < 3$ or $x > 5$

c. $x > 3$ and $x > 5$

d. $x > 3$ or $x > 5$

e. $x > 3$ and $x < 5$

f. $x > 3$ or $x < 5$

10. Write a paragraph about George Boole. Include the years during which he lived, the main logical operators that he studied, and a modern application of his work.

CHAPTER 5

Equivalences and Truth Values

In Chapter 4 you learned that equivalences are biconditionals that are true. This means that when you look at a biconditional you must determine whether it is true. Every biconditional claims to be an equivalence, and it is up to you to expose the false ones.

Some equivalences are especially important because they summarize important rules. An equivalence allows you to substitute the expression on either side for the expression on the other side. So far, you know two equivalences:

$\sim(\sim P) \leftrightarrow P$ **Double Negation (DN)**

$(P \leftrightarrow Q) \leftrightarrow [(P \to Q) \wedge (Q \to P)]$ **Biconditional Rule (BR)**

In this chapter you will prove some other important equivalences. You will also use equivalences to prove new equivalences, which is a convenient shortcut compared to truth tables.

Concepts

For a given implication, $P \to Q$, there are three related implications. The converse, $Q \to P$, was discussed in Chapter 4. The other two related implications are the inverse, $\sim P \to \sim Q$ and the contrapositive, $\sim Q \to \sim P$. Here is a summary.

original implication	$P \to Q$
converse	$Q \to P$
inverse	$\sim P \to \sim Q$
contrapositive	$\sim Q \to \sim P$

In Question 8 of Chapter 4, you made a truth table to prove that the contrapositive means the same as the original implication. Thus,

$P \rightarrow Q$ and $\sim Q \rightarrow \sim P$ are equivalent. This is called the contrapositive rule.

Contrapositive Rule (CR)

$$(P \rightarrow Q) \leftrightarrow (\sim Q \rightarrow \sim P)$$

Here are two other important rules called distributive rules.

Distributive Rules:

Distribution of Disjunction (DD)

$$[P \vee (Q \wedge R)] \leftrightarrow [(P \vee Q) \wedge (P \vee R)]$$

Distribution of Conjunction (DC)

$$[P \wedge (Q \vee R)] \leftrightarrow [(P \wedge Q) \vee (P \wedge R)]$$

The proof of the first of the two distributive rules, distribution of disjunction (DD), will illustrate how to prove the other laws in the questions at the end of the chapter. Neatly write the statement to be proved so that each symbol can be the heading for a column in a truth table. Count the different letters (P, Q, R). Since there are three letters involved, your table must have eight rows. There are twice as many combinations as before since all the previous combinations are possible for both values of the third letter. Fill in the first three lettered columns, P, Q, and R, making sure to list all the combinations. Now fill in the other columns for P in the same order as the first P column. Likewise complete the other Q and R columns so that all columns with the same heading match. Finally, fill in the other columns according to the grouping symbols. Fill in the bold columns, then the circled columns, and then the biconditional (shaded) column. This order requires completing lettered columns first, connectives in parentheses and brackets next, and finally, the main connective.

[P	∨	(Q	∧	R)]	↔	[(P	∨	Q)	∧	(P	∨	R)]
T	T	T	T	T	T	T	T	T	T	T	T	T
T	T	T	F	F	T	T	T	T	T	T	T	F
T	T	F	F	T	T	T	T	F	T	T	T	T
T	T	F	F	F	T	T	T	F	T	T	T	F
F	T	T	T	T	T	F	T	T	T	F	T	T
F	F	T	F	F	T	F	T	T	F	F	F	F
F	F	F	F	T	T	F	F	F	F	F	T	T
F	F	F	F	F	T	F	F	F	F	F	F	F

The biconditional column is always true, since the circled columns have identical truth values. This proves the equivalence of the two expressions.

Negations—You can recognize the negations of each connective from your truth table efforts. Since the conjunction (AND) is false if P or Q is false, $\sim(P \wedge Q)$ means the same as $\sim P \vee \sim Q$. Since disjunction (OR) is false when P and Q are false, $\sim(P \vee Q)$ means $\sim P \wedge \sim Q$. Since an implication is false when P is true and Q is false, $\sim(P \rightarrow Q)$ means $P \wedge \sim Q$. Finally, a biconditional statement is false if exactly one statement is false, so $\sim(P \leftrightarrow Q)$ means $(P \wedge \sim Q) \vee (Q \wedge \sim P)$.

These four new equivalences are summarized below. You may find the two-letter abbreviations helpful in referring to them. The first two are called DeMorgan's rules in honor of their discoverer.

Negation Rules

Negation of Conjunction (NC)

$$\sim(A \wedge B) \leftrightarrow (\sim A \vee \sim B)$$

Negation of Disjunction (ND)

$$\sim(A \vee B) \leftrightarrow (\sim A \wedge \sim B)$$

Negation of Implication (NI)

$$\sim(A \rightarrow B) \leftrightarrow (A \wedge \sim B)$$

Negation of Biconditional (NB)

$$\sim(A \leftrightarrow B) \leftrightarrow [(A \wedge \sim B) \vee (\sim A \wedge B)]$$

You can check all these rules by using truth tables. The truth table below verifies the negation of disjunction rule (ND). You will check the other three negation rules in the questions at the end of this chapter.

[~	(P	∨	Q)	↔	[(~	P)	∧	(~	Q)]
F	T	T	T	T	F	T	F	F	T
F	T	T	F	T	F	T	F	T	F
F	F	T	T	T	T	F	F	F	T
T	F	F	F	T	T	F	T	T	F

Now that you have proved some rules using truth tables, you can prove other rules using the rules already established. This is much quicker than using truth tables. To prove an equivalence, start with one side as given and deduce the other side by making substitutions based on other known equivalences. Since consecutive steps are equivalent, the first and last steps are also equivalent.

Below is the proof of the rule for the negation of a biconditional (NB). Notice that the first step is the left side of the original equivalence and the last step is the other side. Since these steps are equivalent by a series of substitutions, it proves that $[\sim(P \leftrightarrow Q)]$ $\leftrightarrow [(P \land \sim Q) \lor (Q \land \sim P)]$. Using this method, you deduce the negation of a biconditional (NB) in four simple steps instead of a 14-column truth table. See if you understand the substitutions before reading the explanation which follows it.

1. $\sim(P \leftrightarrow Q)$ 1. given
2. $\sim[(P \rightarrow Q) \land (Q \rightarrow P)]$ 2. Biconditional Rule (BR)
3. $[\sim(P \rightarrow Q)] \lor [\sim(Q \rightarrow P)]$ 3. Negation of Conjunction (NC)
4. $(P \land \sim Q) \lor (Q \land \sim P)$ 4. Negation of Implication (NI)

You can start with either side of the equivalence to be proved. The example above takes the left side as given. To obtain Step 2, simply replace $P \leftrightarrow Q$ with its definition [biconditional rule (BR)].

Perhaps Step 3 confused you. Notice that the main connective in Step 2 in the brackets is $\land$ (AND). Therefore, Step 2 has the form $\sim(A \land B)$ where $A = P \rightarrow Q$ and $B = Q \rightarrow P$. Therefore, you must apply the negation of conjunction rule to obtain $\sim A \lor \sim B$. This is what Step 3 says using the same substitutions for A and B.

Now, both brackets contain a negation of an implication. Thus, Step 4 simplifies inside the brackets separately. Apply the negation of implication rule (NI) twice using letter-for-letter substitutions in each bracketed expression.

Applications

Computers—All the compounds can occur in computer programming. Consider a simple seven-line program in BASIC. It greets users and reminds students that they must sign in.

```
100    PRINT "Welcome to the Computer Lab."
200    PRINT "Enter your year in school (1, 2, 3, or 4)."
300    INPUT X
400    IF X < = 4 THEN PRINT "Sign your name at the desk,
       please."
500    IF X > 4 THEN PRINT "The number is not acceptable."
600    IF X < 0 THEN PRINT "The number is not acceptable."
700    END
```

The program is a greeting to someone entering the software. Each numbered line is executed in sequence by the computer. The computer interprets the succession of line numbers as AND. All you do is list each thing to be done. To program a conditional, use the phrase you have studied: "IF . . . THEN." To program the word OR is a bit harder. Notice that in either of two situations (X > 4 or X < 0), the same sentence was printed. This shows that the OR is accomplished by writing the two conditions separately. In more complex computer applications, the words AND, NOT, and OR can be used directly also.

This is just a quick glimpse of the fact that these tools are used in programming. They are also used in *designing* computers. In the questions for Chapter 3, you discovered that T and F are like *on* and *off* for electricity. When a switch is on, the connection is made for current to flow through the wire and "current flows" is true. When the switch is off, the connection is broken and "current flows" is false, since the electricity cannot pass through the wire.

A parallel connection is like the disjunction $A \vee B$, since electricity flows if switch A is on OR if switch B is on.

Parallel Circuit

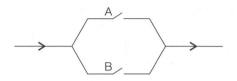

The series connection is like $A \wedge B$, since current flows only when both switches are on.

Series Circuit

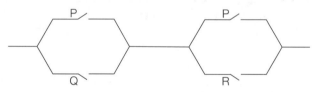

The difference between parallel and series circuits is just like AND and OR.

This relationship helps you to analyze all electrical circuits. You can decide when a circuit is on, and you can also simplify circuits. The circuit shown below has two switches marked P. These must be activated at the same time—both on (T) or both off (F).

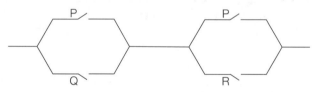

This wiring can be represented by $(P \vee Q) \wedge (P \vee R)$. From the truth table for this expression (see p. 50), you can see that it is on if P is on *or* if both Q and R are on. Furthermore, the distributive rule proves that this expression means the same as $P \vee (Q \wedge R)$. This means that the circuit below is on for exactly the same combinations but requires only three switches instead of four. Using these tools to simplify circuits can save money.

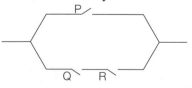

Bible—John 3:16 is *not* an equivalence because it is not even a biconditional. In paraphrase it says "If a person believes in Him [Jesus], then he has everlasting life." This is a good verse for assurance. The converse is "if a person has everlasting life, then he believes in Jesus." The converse shows that there is no other way to everlasting life: Whoever has everlasting life has believed in Jesus. You know that this statement is true, but it is not what John 3:16 says. Thus, if you are discipling a new Christian, use John 3:16 for assurance; however, do not use it to teach that Christ is the only way. Of course, Christ is the only way, but you should teach the point with verses which clearly say that; Acts 4:12 is one such text. However, this reference in Acts would not be used to teach assurance; instead, use John 3:16. In essence, for all spiritual and practical matters, always remember this principle: Do not set a model for teaching truth by twisting grammar.

Some of you will say that this is splitting hairs unnecessarily. You would complain that such nitpicking is reading too much into Scripture and preaching. This criticism should be examined; if it is true, then you should scrap much of this chapter. However, keep two things in mind.

First, there is the matter of trustworthiness. You have learned many truths from the Bible. Some of these truths were taught clearly based on single verses. Hopefully, all were based on proper interpretations of those verses. Do you recall something that you were taught (or that you read) that you thought was true for a while based on a misinterpretation? What happened? You explained what you thought was in the verse. Then someone showed you that you had a wrong idea of a word or that your view was not consistent with other verses. Ultimately you were embarrassed. You had to relearn the principles from other verses. This is frustrating and can make you question the original teacher. Teaching from a converse is setting up your friends for that same embarrassment, frustration, and doubt of your trustworthiness.

Second, there is the matter of courtesy. Imagine that your neighbor hears you say to your child, "Billy, if you ever lie to me, you'll be punished." Several days later you punish Billy for not picking up his toys. While playing with the neighbor's boy, Billy mentions getting his punishment and the neighbor overhears. Later, the neighbor says to you, "I guess your Billy is a real liar." As a parent, that accusation would make you mad and rightfully so. The neighbor jumped to a conclusion. Just because the boy was punished does not mean that he lied. You did not say that lying was the *only* reason for punishment. The neighbor used the converse of your statement, and you know that is not fair, because it does not mean the same as what you said. If it makes you mad, how should God feel when men reverse His conditions? Should we not be as courteous to God with His statements as we expect others to be with ours?

Surely you see this is not splitting hairs. It is important to avoid putting words in people's mouths. It is especially crucial not to speak words in the name of God that He did not say. Use good logic both to show courtesy to God and to be trustworthy interpreters of the Word of God.

Memory Verse—In Chapter 4 you learned that I John 5:12 is an equivalence. This verse asserts both the conditional statement in John 3:16 that Jesus provides salvation and the conditional statement of Acts 4:12 that there is no other way of salvation. You can see how useful such a verse is. Memorize I John 5:12, which gives an equivalence between Jesus Christ and salvation.

Conclusion

Since many equivalences involve three or more letters, their truth tables require many rows. Since the number of rows doubles for each additional letter, a truth table with n different letters must have 2^n rows. You can see that truth tables for an equivalence involving 5 letters would be very long, having 32 rows.

Derivations use sequences of substitutions to prove new equivalences. These save time but require previously proved rules. Therefore, the following equivalences should be learned for convenient reference.

Basic Equivalences

1. Biconditional Rule	$(A \leftrightarrow B) \leftrightarrow [(A \rightarrow B) \wedge (B \rightarrow A)]$
2. Contrapositive Rule	$(A \rightarrow B) \leftrightarrow (\sim B \rightarrow \sim A)$
3. Distribution of Disjunction	$[A \vee (B \wedge C)] \leftrightarrow [(A \vee B) \wedge (A \vee C)]$
4. Distribution of Conjunction	$[A \wedge (B \vee C)] \leftrightarrow [(A \wedge B) \vee (A \wedge C)]$

Negation Rules

5. Negation of Conjunction	$\sim(A \wedge B) \leftrightarrow (\sim A \vee \sim B)$
6. Negation of Disjunction	$\sim(A \vee B) \leftrightarrow (\sim A \wedge \sim B)$
7. Negation of Implication	$\sim(A \rightarrow B) \leftrightarrow (A \wedge \sim B)$
8. Negation of Biconditional	$\sim(A \leftrightarrow B) \leftrightarrow [(A \wedge \sim B) \vee (\sim A \wedge B)]$
9. Double Negation	$\sim(\sim A) \leftrightarrow A.$

Equivalences are important, because they permit one side to be substituted for the other. This helps you do proofs, but it also helps you see the relationship between statements in a discussion. Knowing how to distribute or negate connectives can help you correctly paraphrase statements. You have also seen the relevance of these concepts to computer programming and circuitry as well as to Scripture.

Terms

Biconditional Rule (BR)
contrapositive
Contrapositive Rule (CR)
converse
Distribution of Conjunction Rule (DC)
Distribution of Disjunction Rule (DD)
distributive rules
Double Negation (DN)
inverse
Negation of Biconditional Rule (NB)
Negation of Conjunction Rule (NC)
Negation of Disjunction Rule (ND)
Negation of Implication Rule (NI)
parallel circuit
series circuit

Questions

1. Negate each statement in Question 4 of Chapter 4. Notice that the negations are true only for statements that were originally false.

2. Write the contrapositive rule and then write three other variations of it using your proofs in Question 8 of Chapter 4.

3. Use $S \rightarrow L$ to represent "he that hath the Son hath life." How would you represent the second half of the memory verse? What is it called in relation to $S \rightarrow L$?

4. Explain why I John 5:12 is an equivalence.

5. Use a truth table to show that the following is *not* an equivalence. $(P \rightarrow Q) \leftrightarrow (Q \rightarrow P)$

6. Prove the equivalences using truth tables. (The first three are the ones that the text left for you to check.)

   a. Negation of Conjunction rule (NC)

   b. Negation of Implication rule (NI)

   c. Distribution of Conjunction rule (DC)

   d. Commutative Law for Disjunction:
      $(P \vee Q) \leftrightarrow (Q \vee P)$

   e. Redundancy Rule for Disjunction: $(P \vee P) \leftrightarrow P$

   f. Associative Law for Conjunction:
      $[(P \wedge Q) \wedge R] \leftrightarrow [P \wedge (Q \wedge R)]$

7. Give a reason for each step in the proof of
   $(P \rightarrow Q) \leftrightarrow (\sim P \vee Q)$.

   1. $P \rightarrow Q$
   2. $\sim[\sim(P \rightarrow Q)]$
   3. $\sim[P \wedge \sim Q]$
   4. $\sim P \vee \sim\sim Q$
   5. $\sim P \vee Q$

8. Prove using derivation.
  a. Commutative Law for Conjunction
     $(P \wedge Q) \leftrightarrow (Q \wedge P)$ (Hint: Use Question 6d.)
  b. Associative Law for Disjunction
     $[(P \vee Q) \vee R] \leftrightarrow [P \vee (Q \vee R)]$ (Hint: Use Question 6f.)
  c. Redundancy Rule for Conjunction
     $(P \wedge P) \leftrightarrow P$ (Hint: Use Question 6e.)
  d. $[P \rightarrow (Q \rightarrow R)] \leftrightarrow [(P \wedge Q) \rightarrow R]$
     (Hint: Use the equivalence proved in Question 7.)

9. Circuits and computers:

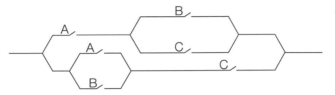

  a. When is the circuit on and off? Use a truth table. Can you find a circuit that uses fewer switches but is on and off in the same circumstances?
  b. According to Question 8d, how could you program the following idea? If $(X > 3$ and $X \neq 10)$, then let $Y = 8$.

10. Write a paragraph about Augustus DeMorgan. Include biographical information and comment on DeMorgan's Laws. What were these laws called in this chapter?

CHAPTER 6
Arguments by Induction

What is an argument anyway? An **argument** is a sequence of statements (called **premises**) that are intended to establish the truth of another statement (called the **conclusion**). Arguments are not loud and heated disputes. Calling someone names is not an argument because no premises are given to support a conclusion. The definition shows that the sentences must be statements, and there must be intent to show why the conclusion is true. Consider the following sequence of sentences.

Mars is green.
Ice cream is a mineral.
Therefore, oaks grow naturally only in Florida.

Is this an argument? Yes! the first two sentences are statements. "Oaks grow naturally only in Florida" is also a statement. Remember that statements may or may not be true. The word *therefore* is a clue that the last statement is intended as a conclusion drawn from the first two statements. The definition said only that there must be intent to prove the conclusion, not that the truth of the conclusion must be established.

You can see that there are bad arguments as well as good ones. Your goal throughout the rest of the book is to learn to decide when an argument is good and when it is not. Since you are dealing with collections of statements, all your work with true and false compounds in the previous two chapters will become very helpful. Since every argument (and every statement) consists of words, the first two chapters of this book form the building blocks for all other chapters.

You use arguments every day. Every time someone asks you "Why?" he is asking you to argue in support of a statement you previously made. Every time you ask someone "Why?" you are asking him to support his position.

When you ask "Why?" you will have to evaluate the strength of the answer. When you are asked "Why?" your own argument will be scrutinized for weaknesses by your hearers. This means that your constructions of arguments and your evaluations of arguments are important and influence your decisions every day.

As you study the principles of good and bad arguments, your abilities to correctly evaluate and construct arguments should improve. You will apply these principles every time you answer a question, whether verbally or in writing, with friends or in class.

In this chapter and the next, you will study basic types of good arguments. In Chapters 8 and 9, you will look at some complex kinds of arguments and in Chapters 10 and 11, you will look at common mistakes in arguments. Please study this chapter and the next carefully. You will see that understanding the remaining chapters depends on a proper understanding of these basics.

Concepts

There are two basic types of arguments: inductive and deductive. This chapter will focus on good inductive arguments. Deductive arguments will be discussed in the next chapter. But what is the difference?

An **inductive argument** is one that intends to show that the conclusion is probable or most likely. A **deductive argument** intends to prove that the conclusion must be true. Here are examples of each:

> Inductive: Dr. Trench has performed 100 lung transplants and all were successful. When Dr. Trench transplants a lung for Aunt Cathy, it will be successful.

> Deductive: All gerbils are rodents. All rodents are mammals. Therefore, all gerbils are mammals.

Both of these arguments are good, but there is a difference. The deductive argument is foolproof. There are no logical holes, and it is always true: every gerbil is a mammal. The inductive argument presents very good evidence but could still be false. It is possible for Dr. Trench to make a mistake, even though he has succeeded so far. His good track record does make it unlikely, though, and the conclusion is founded on good solid evidence. Really, you would probably rather go to Dr. Trench than to Dr. Crackpot, who just finished medical school and is about to do his first transplant.

Different words are used to describe good arguments of these different types. It is possible that the reasoning or form of argument is correct but that one of the premises is false. In the above example, what if Dr. Trench has never performed a lung transplant? The reasoning is still good, but the basic premise is false. This shows that you will have to evaluate the truth of the premises separately from the correctness of the reasoning.

If the reasoning is correct (whether or not the premises are true), the inductive argument is **strong** (not "certain" or "valid," since it only shows likelihood). If the reasoning provides little or no support, it is **weak**. A good inductive argument is one that displays strong reasoning and true premises. These are called **cogent**. If the inductive argument has false premises or is weak, it is **uncogent**.

There are six basic ways to make a strong argument. For evidence you may appeal to authority, utility, experience, silence, analogy, or tendency. Illustrations of each of these methods follow.

Authority—An **appeal to authority** is strong if the authority is qualified. If Michael Jordan says that a certain type of basketball play is effective against a zoned defense, his statement may properly be used as evidence. On the other hand, if he recommends a certain brand of tennis racket, the argument is less convincing, since he is not an authority on tennis.

Remember that the Bible is the only infallible authority. It is still possible to construct weak appeals even from the Bible, though, because the statement may be misused or twisted in meaning by the arguer. Except for proper use of biblical authority, argument based on authority is the least convincing of the six methods of inductive argumentation.

Utility—An **appeal to utility** is an argument supporting a conclusion based on the fact that it works. This type of appeal can be strong, such as when you learn a shortcut computation in math. Many people use the rule that a number is divisible by three if the sum of the digits is divisible by three. For instance, 537 is divisible by 3 because $5 + 3 + 7 = 15$ and $15 \div 3$ is 5. Most of the people who use the rule have no idea why it works, but they know that it does work because they can check their answers ($537 \div 3 = 179$).

Appeals to utility are strong if they meet two criteria. First, the method should not require anything false, deceptive, morally wrong, or otherwise unbiblical. Second, it should work in representative instances and have no obvious exception. A person could multiply 0×5 and come out with the right answer for $\frac{0}{5}$. If the person tried to say dividing is the same as multiplying because it works, he would have a weak argument. The fact that $0 \times 5 = \frac{0}{5}$ is not representative; in fact, $4 \times 2 = 8$, but $\frac{4}{2} = 2$.

Experience—If a man said he saw God in person last night, would you believe him? I hope not. The Bible plainly states that "no man hath seen God at any time" (I John 4:12). Assuming he is not intentionally lying, the man may have dreamed or hallucinated; nonetheless, his experience is not proof.

In contrast, an **appeal to experience** can be strong. Imagine that while shopping for cars, three friends who each owned the same model told you what great mileage they got, how dependable the car was, and that it needed no repairs in five years. You certainly would give that model consideration. The Bible also says "in the multitude of counsellors there is safety" (Prov. 11:14).

Experience can be strong evidence if properly used. In a court of law, there must be testimonies of more than one person. The testimonies must relate experiences consistent with each other (otherwise the testimonies are inconsistent—conflicting statements). Each experience must also be coherent and hold together (otherwise the witness is incoherent—a lunatic).

Matthew 18 reinforces this idea by explaining the need of two or three witnesses when presenting accusations against another person. Several consistent testimonies of eyewitness experiences demonstrate as much as possible the truth of the accusation.

Silence—Arguments from silence are usually not considered strong. There is a good reason for this. Consider this attack on the book of Esther in the Old Testament: The name of God is not found in the book of Esther, and so the writer did not believe in God. This argument uses the silence of the book on a subject as evidence against the subject. This argument is weak. A writer does not have to write about everything he believes in every book he writes.

There are situations, though, when an **appeal to silence** is strong. In a court of law the rule is "innocent until proven guilty." If no evidence can be found, this absence supports the person's innocence. Innocence is defended by an argument from silence. There is lack of evidence of guilt.

If many tests are made on a person to see if he has cancer and all the tests are negative, the person does not have cancer. This silence (lack of a positive test for cancer) provides evidence of good health.

There are many good arguments from silence. Such an argument is strong if the lack of evidence is persistent. A continuous pattern of silence is significant unless it can be accounted for otherwise (as with the Esther argument); however, an argument from silence should not be used if another method is applicable.

Analogy—An **appeal to analogy** compares two things. One of the things is obviously true and is similar to the second. The similarity is used to support the truth of the desired conclusion about the second thing. This method requires the two things to be comparable.

Clear examples of analogy arguments are found often in the Bible. Jesus often used analogy. One example is found in Luke 13:15-16. After Jesus healed a stooped woman, the ruler of the synagogue accused Him of violating the Sabbath. Jesus replied by analogy. He asked him if he had ever untied an ox to let it drink water on the Sabbath. This analogy presents an obvious truth; the ruler knew that every ox owner had to do this and none were ever accused of working on the Sabbath. Jesus went on to say that if the ox (a beast) can be freed on the Sabbath, then one of God's chosen people can be freed also. The comparison is strong. People are more valuable than beasts, so releasing a woman from satanic binding on God's day of rest is much more reasonable than releasing an ox from human binding on God's day of rest.

Suppose Bobby Tate says to his dad:

"Davey Price gets to stay out until midnight every night.
Can I stay out that late too?"

Of course, this analogy is weak. The two families are very different. Davey's father may be unsaved, and he may think Davey needs to learn primarily by experience. Perhaps Davey's parents are never home and, for this reason, Davey is just as jealous of Bobby who has caring parents. Perhaps Davey has proven to be more responsible and has earned the privilege. Have you ever made the mistake Bobby made?

Comparisons should be made from the main point of the analogy only. When this rule is ignored, the comparison seems unreasonable. For instance, policemen should not be compared to murderers.

Tendency—This method and the analogy method are the two strongest methods of inductive argument when used properly. In an **appeal to tendency** the conclusion summarizes a pattern that has been noticed. This conclusion is a **generalization** from the instances. To use this method properly, you must have many observed instances in a wide variety of representative contexts. This is the way that many scientific principles are discovered; it is also how predictions of elections are made.

Consider an election. If three of your friends say that they are going to vote for Sam Landon, that does not mean Landon will win. Your three friends are not representative of all voters. If you randomly survey 100 people on a street corner, your generalization is much stronger. For a mayoral election, the results of a street corner survey would be a strong argument, but for a national election it is weak because that city may not be representative of the nation. Furthermore, even in the city election, if Landon wins the survey by a margin of 53% to 47%, the prediction of a Landon victory is still weak because the pattern does not display a significant lead.

You may ask how much of a margin is needed? Would a 59% to 41% lead be enough? 70% to 30%? Or do you need a margin as high as 90% to 10%? The answers to these questions depend on how many people were surveyed. You can more accurately predict the winner of a close race if you survey millions of voters. The number of people you survey is the **sample size.** The science of statistics tells you the appropriate sample size for given percentage margins. This book will use only clear margins like 90% to 10% to illustrate a strong argument.

Appeals to tendency, then, must meet two criteria. First, the tendency or pattern must be clear. Second, the sample must be representative.

Applications

English—Look at the words in List 1. Can you appeal to tendency to draw a generalization about spelling?

List 1
tie
cried
flies
friend
field
yield
applied
incipient
sieve
grieve
believe
wield
siege
pier
pierce
piety
soldier
science
conscience
chiefs
quiet
babies

List 2
beige
neighbor
reindeer
reign
weigh
veil
their
deceive
receive
reinforce
weird
seizure

The pattern that you should notice for spelling is that "*i* comes before *e*." This is a strong conclusion. There is a wide variety of words; they do not all rhyme; the number of syllables varies, and various letters precede and follow *ie*.

Now consider List 2. Since there are many exceptions to the generalization based on List 1, was the generalization weak after all? Not really. Generalizations in spelling are bound to have exceptions, and the pattern did work for many words. Of course, a stronger generalization could be made. In the first seven words of List 2, the *ei* sounds like long *a*. This sound never occurs as *ie* in List 1. In the next two words in List 2, the *ei* follows *c*. The word *reinforce* does not follow the *ie* pattern, because the vowels are pronounced separately. The separate pronunciation is due to its formation from *enforce* by adding a prefix.

Generalization: *i* before *e* except after *c* or when sounding like "ay" as in *neighbor* and *weigh* (or when the vowels are pronounced separately)." Perhaps you noticed that *science* and *conscience* do not follow the *i* before *e* except after *c* rule. However, you can see that the vowels are pronounced separately in *science*. Also, *conscience* is formed from *science* by adding the prefix *con,* so it retains the same spelling as *science* even though the vowels are not pronounced separately. Thus, these exceptions can be viewed as covered by the note on separate vowel pronunciation.

This generalization is very strong but still has two exceptions, *weird* and *seizure*. These rare exceptions do not warrant modification of the generalization.

Inductive arguments are used not only in spelling but also in finding main points and themes in stories and essays. This method of reasoning is demonstrated in the book of Jude. The first thing you must look for is repetition. Looking through Jude for patterns of related words or topics, you find specific patterns as presented in the table on the following page:

be on guard	evil men	sin	punishment
contend (v. 3)	ungodly (v. 4)	fornication (v. 7)	destroyed (v. 5)
remembrance (v. 5)	filthy dreamers (v. 8)	corrupt them-selves (v. 10)	judgment (v. 6)
contending (v. 9)	spots (v. 12)	ungodly deeds (v. 15)	eternal fire (v. 7)
remember (v. 17)	ungodly sinners (v. 15)	their own lusts (v.16)	woe (v. 11)
building up yourselves (v. 20)	murmurers (v. 16)	ungodly lusts (v. 18)	perished (v. 11)
keep yourselves (v. 21)	complainers (v.16)	sensual (v. 19)	twice dead (v. 12)
to keep you from falling (v. 24)	mockers (v.18)		darkness for ever (v. 13)
			judgment (v. 15)
			the fire (v. 23)

These patterns show that there are four recurring ideas in the book of Jude. The recurring ideas indicate minor themes, major themes, and the primary (main) theme of the book. To determine the main theme, compare the points made about each topic and look for a pattern. Examining each topic in Jude, you see that the point about "evil men" and "sin" in verses 4-16 is that such people and practices are punished by God. The evil men involved in sin in verses 18-19 contrast with how the believers should live. Believers should guard against sin. This suggests that the "evil men" and "sin" topics support the other two points.

1. Believers should be on guard against evil men and their deeds (sins).

2. Punishment will come upon evil men and their deeds (sins).

How do you make the final decision between these two possible themes? Review the book observing the patterns again.

The greeting mentions neither topic (vv. 1-2). The first verse after the greeting says "ye should earnestly contend for the faith." This involves warning to be on guard against the evil men and sins in the subsequent verses. The punishments emphasize results of evil and serve as warnings. Verses 20-23, also, primarily command the readers to strive to stay strong in the Lord. The closing two verses do not mention punishment, but attribute to God the ability to keep believers from falling into these evils. Since only the first statement (statement 1 above) ties the whole book together, you can argue from tendency that the first statement is the main theme. So verse 3 should be considered the key verse. Contend for the faith!

Having identified the theme by appeal to tendency, you should also recognize that Jude's own argument showing the need to contend is itself an appeal to tendency—and a cogent one at that! Notice that more than six examples are given, demonstrating a clear pattern and providing representative examples. The examples provide a representative sample of types of persons who need to guard against sin: God's people, the Jews (v. 5); the angels (v. 6); and also the Gentiles (v. 7). Other examples give a variety of sins to guard against: Cain's stubborn pride, Balaam's greed, and Core's gainsaying (v. 11). Jude offers quite an impressive model of an inductive argument.

Science—Weather forecasting (meteorology) is of course based on appeals to tendency. Past weather patterns form the basis of all predictions.

Appeals to silence are used in medical research. Many new potential cures are first tested on rodents or primates. When a medicine does not cause a change in the blood pressure of lab rodents, researchers conclude that the medicine does not affect the blood pressure of any rodents. Notice the appeal to silence. Next, the researcher argues by analogy. He reasons that the medicine will not affect human blood pressure either because of the similarity of the human circulatory system to that of the animals tested.

Many a student has memorized the list of major elements needed for plant growth (macronutrients) using the mnemonic "See Hopkins Cafe, Mighty Good." This helps them to remember the list C HOPK'NS CaFe Mg. These letters are the chemical symbols for the elements they need to know (carbon, hydrogen, oxygen, phosphorus, potassium, nitrogen, sulfur, calcium, iron, magnesium). Why should they learn the mnemonic? Certainly, the imaginary restaurant has nothing to do with plant nutrition. The only reason for learning it is that it works. That is, utility supplies the method of justification for most mnemonic devices.

Of course, science has many other uses for induction. The most important ones have not been addressed, because they are much more complex. These will be presented in Chapter 8.

Bible—You have already examined two uses of induction in the Bible. The book of Jude urges the readers to contend for the faith based on the generalization from examples of judgment for not doing so.

Jesus uses analogies very often. You found one example of the Lord's analogies in Luke 13:15-16. Paul also uses analogies as you will see shortly. (See memory verse for this chapter.)

Jesus also frequently appeals to authority. The authority is always the Scripture. In Matthew 22:32, Jesus quotes Exodus 3:6. This quote serves as the basis of His argument against the Sadducees.

Peter argues from experience in II Peter 1:16-18. He gives evidence that Jesus had really lived on earth by sharing his experience as an eyewitness (v. 16). He was with Jesus (v. 18). Peter goes on to say that the authority of Scripture is a stronger argument than his experience. Nevertheless, Peter's argument from experience is not to be ignored—the Spirit inspired his argument. Another argument from experience in the Bible is given by John in the opening of his first epistle.

Memory Verse—I Corinthians 9:9-10

"For it is written in the law of Moses, Thou shalt not muzzle the mouth of the ox that treadeth out the corn. Doth God take care for oxen? Or saith he it altogether for our sakes? For our sakes, no doubt, this is written: that he that ploweth should plow in hope; and that he that thresheth in hope should be partaker of his hope."

Here Paul quotes the Old Testament law prohibiting muzzling an ox so that it cannot eat while treading. If Paul were confronting a farmer who muzzled his ox, the Old Testament reference would be a simple appeal to biblical authority to unmuzzle the ox. Instead, though, he argues a principle: the ox can partake of its labor; in like manner (by analogy) every worker can partake of his labor. This principle is emphasized again in verse 14 (and v. 13). "They which preach the gospel should live of the gospel.'' Paul is arguing for the right of preachers to be supported by their churches, and his argument is by analogy. He says that even as an ox is guaranteed by God the right to be supported by his work, how much more should people in God's work!

Conclusion

This chapter first defined *argument* and then classified arguments as inductive or deductive. The chapter stressed the classifications and criteria for good inductive arguments.

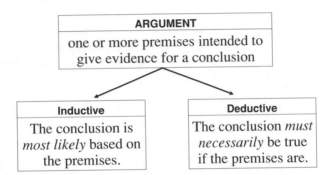

The next chapter presents the types of deductive arguments. Here is the list of the types of inductive arguments:

1. appeal to authority
2. appeal to utility
3. appeal to experience
4. appeal to silence
5. appeal to analogy
6. appeal to tendency

Inductive reasoning is strong or weak. The premises of an inductive argument are true or false. A strong inductive argument with true premises is cogent; otherwise, it is uncogent.

These ideas have far-reaching application. Everyone uses them daily whenever he gives or requests the reasons for something. Your communication will be clearer and above reproach if you understand and use proper inductive techniques.

Specific applications to English, science, and the Bible were noted. Use these ideas to find the theme of any piece of literature, to learn principles of spelling, to understand science, and to understand and apply the Bible.

Terms

appeal to analogy
appeal to authority
appeal to experience
appeal to silence
appeal to tendency
appeal to utility
argument
cogent
conclusion
deductive argument
inductive argument
premises
sample size
strong
uncogent
weak

Questions

1. Complete the following charts.
   a. For each combination of premises and reasoning, decide whether the argument is cogent or uncogent.

		Reasoning	
		Strong	Weak
Premises	True		
	False		

b. For each combination of reasoning and argument, decide if the premises are true or not.

		Argument	
		Cogent	Uncogent
Reasoning	Strong		
	Weak		

c. For each combination of premises and argument, decide whether the reasoning is strong or weak.

		Argument	
		Cogent	Uncogent
Premises	True		
	False		

2. Which method of induction is used in each argument below?

   a. Luke 18:1-8

   b. Hebrews 11 (Use v. 1 as the conclusion.)

   c. Acts 1:20-22

   d. I Corinthians 15:32

3. The arguments below attempt to convince Joe to accept Christ. Which method of induction is used in each? Each method is used only once.

   a. ''Joe, I know you are going through a lot of hard times and you just want peace. You should trust Jesus as Savior because He will give you that peace.''

   b. ''Joe, I have never known anyone that trusted Jesus to be sorry for doing so. If you trust Him, Joe, you will not regret it.''

   c. ''Joe, the Bible says 'Believe on the Lord Jesus Christ and thou shalt be saved'; so if *you* believe, you will be saved too!''

   d. ''Joe, you know that I was a sinner just like you, and you know God has changed my life. He can change yours too!''

e. "Joe, no one can be saved by doing good. Abraham believed God; David asked forgiveness; Martha said 'I believe that thou art the Christ'; the eunuch said 'I believe that Jesus Christ is the Son of God'; and Paul, the chief of sinners, was saved by faith."

f. "Joe, God saved me. I am not special, and I am not good, but I'm a sinful man. Yet Jesus died to save even me."

4. Complete the following arguments from tendency. Draw a generalization about mammals. If the argument is not cogent, explain why not.

a. Giraffes give birth to living young. Dogs also produce living offspring. Mice, lions, porcupines, and whales all bear living young. Therefore, . . .

b. A moose has hair. An elk also has hair. Therefore, . . .

c. Seals, lions, bats, dogs, deer, buffalo, and mice are all carnivorous. Therefore, . . .

d. Whales give milk. Bats, wolves, monkeys, and elephants also give milk. Even cougars, cats, and cattle give milk. Therefore, . . .

5. Complete each argument by making a statement about life on other planets. Decide which form of argument you used and decide if it is cogent. If it is not cogent, explain why not.

a. I saw a UFO. Therefore, . . .

b. My doctor saw a UFO. Therefore, . . .

c. The Bible says that God created life on earth and gave man rule over *all* life. Therefore, . . .

d. God created Earth, and He made life on it. God also created other planets. Therefore, . . .

e. Hundreds of extraterrestrials have been interviewed by teams of expert psychologists, biologists, and political leaders. Therefore, . . .

f. No extraterrestrial life has ever been clearly documented or photographed. Therefore, . . .

g. Existence of Martians is helpful in explaining the reports of sightings of mysterious objects. Therefore, . . .

Note: This chapter discussed generalizations from words to rules of English spelling. In the next two questions, you will make generalizations from sentences to rules of grammar.

6. Compare each of the sentences below to the first. How is word position within a sentence used in English?

   a. John swiftly rowed his red canoe toward the dock.

   b. His red canoe John swiftly rowed toward the dock.

   c. The dock John swiftly rowed his red canoe toward.

   d. Toward the dock John swiftly rowed his red canoe.

   e. Swiftly, John rowed his red canoe toward the dock.

   f. Rowed John his red canoe swiftly toward the dock.

7. Each sentence below has an adverb. Can you write a rule for the normal placement of adverbs in English sentences? Expect exceptions! In fact, question 6 suggests an explanation for one exception.

   a. John never denied his Lord.

   b. Children should immediately obey their parents.

   c. Pat gave Bill a bicycle later.

   d. I saw Jane again.

   e. Mona fixes her eyes often on the pastries.

   f. Jesus abides with His saints forever.

   g. Sandy quietly slept for ten hours.

   h. Twice I prayed to God for strength.

   i. Ben has never arrived at work on time.

   j. Jack lives in the jungle dangerously among the cannibals.

8. Scott conducted a job satisfaction survey. He stood on a busy street corner at noon and asked every fifth person walking by to fill out a short questionnaire. One question requested them to give their business hours. No respondents claimed to work from midnight to 5 A.M. Scott was surprised that in such a large city there were no night-shift workers. What is wrong with Scott's reasoning?

9. Using the Gospels, find three more examples of appeal to analogy in the teachings of Jesus.

10. Write a paragraph on Peter Abelard and his contributions to logic.

CHAPTER 7

Arguments by Deduction

Recall that a deductive argument is an argument in which the conclusion *must* follow from the premises. In this chapter you will learn seven basic types of deductive argument. Just as there are both good and bad inductive arguments, so there are both good and bad deductive arguments. A deductive argument may be bad because of either faulty reasoning or a false premise, just as with inductive arguments. If a deductive argument displays good reasoning, it is **valid.** A valid argument with true premises is **sound.** Note that *sound* is to *valid* as *cogent* is to *strong*. The only difference is whether the argument is deductive or inductive. Deductive arguments are sound, but inductive arguments are strong. Since deductive conclusions *must* follow, they are either wholly correct or wholly incorrect. *Valid* and *sound* are not comparative terms like *strong* and *cogent*. Talking about valid inductive arguments or strong deductions results in the same kind of confusion as saying "the boats galloped" and "the horses sailed." Be careful of your terminology! As you study these arguments, you will use truth tables and derivations to aid understanding. You may want to review these principles in the conclusion of Chapter 5.

Concepts

Modus ponens—This is perhaps the most basic type of deductive argument. *Modus ponens* applies a general rule to a specific case. Compare the argument below to the set diagram.

All dogs are mammals.	(general rule)
Rover is a dog.	(specific rule)
Therefore, Rover is a mammal.	(application)

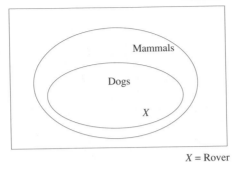

Universe

X = Rover

To emphasize the conditional form of the first statement, use the paraphrase below: (the symbol for "therefore" is $\therefore$).

If it is a dog, then it is a mammal.	$D \rightarrow M$
It is a dog.	D
Therefore, it is a mammal.	$\therefore M$

It may be possible to argue about the premises—perhaps Rover is a canary. But it is *not* possible to argue that the reasoning is bad. This is a valid argument, but it is sound only if Rover really is a dog.

The first premise is a conditional statement ($P \rightarrow Q$). The second premise is the statement P that affirms the "if" part (hypothesis). Both parts are needed to guarantee the conclusion, Q. You can translate this into symbols by noting that the implication *and* the hypothesis together *guarantee* the conclusion. The truth table for the translation appears below. Remember to fill in the P and Q columns first and then complete the remaining columns according to grouping symbols.

Conditional Statement			Together with	Hypothesis of Conditional	Guarantee	Conclusion
[(P	$\rightarrow$	Q)	$\wedge$	P]	$\rightarrow$	Q
T	T	T	**T**	T	T	T
T	F	F	**F**	T	T	F
F	T	T	**F**	F	T	T
F	T	F	**F**	F	T	F

This argument is always true. You have seen this exemplified in diagram form and proved using a truth table.

Notice that this is not an equivalence (substitution rule). It can be used only in one direction. Q can be derived from two statements $P \rightarrow Q$ and P, but the two statements cannot be derived from Q.

This illustrates the difference between the substitution rules of Chapter 4 and the new rules of which *modus ponens* is the first. Both lists are important, but do not confuse them. Argument forms are not the same as equivalent statements. The difference is between drawing a conclusion and paraphrasing.

You studied ***modus ponens*** (**MP**) first because it is very basic. Remember, every time you take a general principle and apply it to a specific case, you are using this rule. Now consider the other six forms of argument.

Modus tollens—Diagram this argument.

All dogs are mammals.

Speedy is not a mammal.

Therefore, Speedy is not a dog.

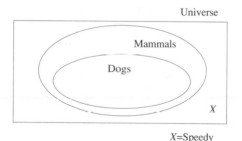

Universe

X=Speedy

Since the dog circle is inside the mammal circle and Speedy is outside, it is impossible for Speedy to be a dog. This argument illustrates ***modus tollens*** (**MT**). To prove it you will need to symbolize the argument. Do you see the form for *modus tollens*?

$P \rightarrow Q$
$\underline{\sim Q}$
$\therefore \sim P$

For the proof, you could make a truth table similar to the one done for *modus ponens*. However, as with equivalences, it is quicker to prove it using a derivation. Both previously proved arguments and equivalences can be used in the proof. Study the sequence of steps below.

1. $P \to Q$	1. given
2. $\sim Q$	2. given
3. $\sim Q \to \sim P$	3. contrapositive rule used on Step 1
4. $\sim P$	4. *Modus ponens* argument with Steps 2 and 3 as premises

Steps 1 and 2 are given (as premises always are). Step 3 is a substitution using an equivalence rule from Chapter 4. Step 4 uses *modus ponens*. To see this, compare:

$$A \to B \qquad \sim Q \to \sim P$$
$$\underline{A} \qquad\qquad \underline{\sim Q}$$
$$\therefore B \qquad\quad \therefore\ \sim P$$

You see that the statement, $\sim Q$, appears both as a premise and as the hypothesis of the conditional. According to *modus ponens*, when these two are the same, the conclusion follows. In this case the conclusion is $\sim P$. This illustrates that the letters in argument forms are placeholders. You can substitute any expression for each letter. Just as $A = \sim Q$ and $B = \sim P$ in the *modus ponens* argument above, the following argument also illustrates *modus ponens*.

$$[(K \wedge L) \leftrightarrow J] \to (S \vee \sim F)$$
$$\underline{(K \wedge L) \leftrightarrow J}$$
$$\therefore S \vee \sim F$$

The name **syllogism** refers to any argument having two premises and a conclusion (three statements total). Both *modus ponens* and *modus tollens* are syllogisms. Here is another syllogism.

Disjunctive Syllogism—This type of argument uses the process of elimination on two choices. Here is an example:

A premise is either true or false	$A \vee B$
The premise is not true.	$\underline{\sim A}$
Therefore, the premise is false.	$\therefore B$

You probably recall many times when this kind of reasoning is used ("Either stop fighting or go to your rooms." "You did not stop fighting," therefore . . .). A **disjunctive syllogism (DS)** is simply a syllogism having a disjunction as one of its premises. You will prove the validity of disjunctive syllogisms using both a truth table and a derivation in Questions 2 and 3.

Transitivity Argument—See if you can symbolize the argument below.

All poodles are dogs.

All dogs are mammals.

Therefore, all poodles are mammals.

The diagram below should help you accept this simple syllogism. A **transitivity argument (TA)** always diagrams like this.

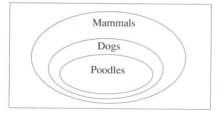

The symbolic form will help you when you prove it. This syllogism is proved in Question 1.

$$P \rightarrow D$$
$$D \rightarrow M$$
$$\therefore \ P \rightarrow M$$

Conjunctive Syllogism—Of course, a **conjunctive syllogism (CS)** is a syllogism in which one statement (the conclusion) is a conjunction.

The car has brakes.

The car has headlights.

Therefore, the car has both brakes and headlights.

A more interesting example is based on the definition of disjunctive syllogism:

The argument is a syllogism.	A
The argument uses a disjunction.	B
Therefore, the argument is a disjunctive syllogism.	$A \wedge B$

This syllogism can be proved easily. In fact, it says simply that $(A \wedge B) \rightarrow (A \wedge B)$. Not only is this conditional true, it is also an equivalence.

Simplification Argument—This is perhaps the most obvious form of argument. You can emphasize an aspect of something known. It is called a **simplification argument (SA)** because you simplify the known information to get down to the point to be emphasized.

Rover is a blind puppy.	$A \wedge B$
Therefore, Rover is blind.	$\therefore A$

The premise means "Rover is blind *and* Rover is a puppy." The word *and* is the key. When two things are known, either can be concluded. This is *not* a syllogism but can be proved easily because it is the converse of the obvious equivalence mentioned in the section on conjunctive syllogism above.

Addition Argument—Finally, when something is known, any disjunction may be formed from it.

Rover is a puppy.	A
Therefore, Rover is a puppy *or* Rover is a platypus.	$\therefore A \vee B$

The name **addition argument (AA)** should help you remember that you can add statements with disjunctions. The conclusion above is more commonly expressed, "Rover is a puppy or a platypus." Any disjunction is true if one part is true. Since Rover is a puppy, you can even correctly conclude, "Rover is a puppy, or the moon is made of green cheese."

You can see that this is not a syllogism either since there is only one premise. Symbolize the argument $A \rightarrow (A \vee B)$. The truth table below proves the argument since the implication is always true.

A	→	(A	∨	B)
T	**T**	T	T	T
T	**T**	T	T	F
F	**T**	F	T	T
F	**T**	F	F	F

Applications

Logic—The principles thus far covered can be very helpful in evaluating discussions. Of course, with practice you should not need to write everything down to recognize a valid or invalid argument, but that will not reduce the value of these tools. Consider this specific argument:

> You can reduce guilt by seeing a psychologist, but you must confess your sin to God to be free of it, or perhaps you could be free of guilt if you ignore it. All of us have tried to ignore guilt and the only result is more guilt feelings. Therefore, the proper action is either to get saved or to confess sin.

First, translate the argument into symbols. You can do this by assigning letters to each statement and combining them with connectives. The argument requires only five letters because "more guilt" can be represented as the negation of "freedom from guilt."

P = visit a psychologist to reduce guilt

C = confess sin to God to be free from it

I = ignore sin

F = be free of sin

S = get saved.

$(P \wedge C) \vee (I \rightarrow F)$

$\underline{I \wedge \sim F}$

$\therefore S \vee C$

Second, decide how to evaluate it. If the argument seems unreasonable or if you are very unsure, you should make a truth table. Truth tables provide the only method so far for showing that an argument is not valid (not always a true conditional). The disadvantage is that this could take a long time. The argument above has 5 letters, so the truth table will have 32 rows ($2^5 = 32$) for each of the 16 columns. If the argument seems reasonable, or if the only thing that sounds suspect is a premise, then you should try to derive it to show that the reasoning is valid. This is much quicker. You will learn more tools for this in later chapters as well as ways to identify false reasoning.

Third, implement your method of evaluation. If you cannot finish a proof, you may need to switch methods and try again.

1.	$(P \wedge C) \vee (I \to F)$	1.	premise
2.	$I \wedge \sim F$	2.	premise
3.	$(I \to F) \vee (P \wedge C)$	3.	Commutative Law for Disjunction (from Step 1)
4.	$\sim(I \to F)$	4.	Negation of Implication (from Step 2)
5.	$P \wedge C$	5.	Disjunctive Syllogism (Steps 3 and 4 as premises)
6.	$C \wedge P$	6.	Commutative Law for Conjunction (from Step 5)
7.	C	7.	Simplification Argument (Step 6 as premise)
8.	$C \vee S$	8.	Addition Argument (Step 7 as premise)
9.	$S \vee C$	9.	Commutative Law for Disjunction (from Step 8)

Since Step 9 is the conclusion, this shows that the conclusion really does follow from the premises. The argument is valid. A person who disagrees has no option but to disagree with one or both of the premises. With practice you should be able to apply the commutative rules (laws) in your head without getting confused. This will permit you to write less (skip Steps 3, 6, and 9). Eventually, you may be able to correctly identify it as a valid modification of disjunctive syllogism just by looking at it.

Test-taking—These rules of logic are effectively used in multiple choice and true-false questions. On true-false items, each one is either true or false ($T \vee F$). If you read a question and suspect that it is not exactly true ($\sim T$), then you must conclude that it is false. This is a simple disjunctive syllogism.

The same is true on multiple choice items. Imagine that there are four choices ($A \vee B \vee C \vee D$). Sometimes you know the answer instantly and you can look for it among the options. Consider the following mutiple-choice question:

George Washington was the first
   A. sultan of the District of Columbia.
   B. supreme court justice of the United States.
   C. president of the United States.
   D. mayor of New York.

No special reasoning takes place to identify C as the answer. On the other hand, sometimes you will not know the answer and must evaluate the options. Consider the next multiple-choice statement:

War was declared on Vietnam by
   A. John D. Rockefeller.
   B. L. B. Johnson.
   C. Winston Churchill.
   D. Woodrow Wilson.

Here, even if you are in doubt, you can narrow the possibilities. Churchill is British, and Great Britain was not in the war; Rockefeller was not a president and had no power to declare war. Now there are only two possibilities. Now you can guess B or D—at least you are making an educated guess and doing your best by avoiding the two worst options. However, on reflection, you may remember that Wilson lived quite a while before Johnson and was president too early for the Vietnam War. Perhaps their order escapes you, but you recall that there was a positive outlook during Wilson's time, but not during the Vietnam conflict. Either way, you can correctly narrow your choice to B.

How was this a disjunctive syllogism? Knowing that $\vee$ is commutative and associative, organize the four options this way:

$C \vee [A \vee (D \vee B)]$

Now you can see in symbols how the process of elimination was a chain of disjunctive syllogisms.

$C \vee [A \vee (D \vee B)]$

$\underline{\sim C}$ _____ not Churchill

$A \vee (D \vee B)$

$\underline{\sim A}$ _____ not Rockefeller

$D \vee B$

$\underline{\sim D}$ _____ not Wilson

B

Each time you eliminated one possibility, you used a disjunctive syllogism. Then you took the remaining possibilities and constructed another disjunctive syllogism until it was down to one possibility: the answer.

The hardest matching problems—the ones in which answers can be used more than once—are really just a set of multiple-choice problems with the same set of options. For matching questions in which answers are used just once, every time you identify one match, the number of selections for your next "multiple choice" decreases. This tells you that your first matches should be the ones you are most certain about; otherwise, you may eliminate options needed later.

Math—Math both requires and develops many logic skills with a special emphasis on deduction. That is why most people think of math problems as right or wrong (remember deduction means the conclusion must follow from true premises). Mathematical truth is often discovered by induction, but then each truth is proved by deduction. Learning good use of deduction in math is important, since you have seen how often you need deduction in every area of life. Study these representative examples.

1. Find x in the following right triangle, $\triangle ABC$.

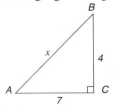

To solve for x, use the Pythagorean theorem ($a^2 + b^2 = c^2$). Applying this theorem requires *modus ponens*.

(1) If a triangle is a right triangle, then $a^2 + b^2 = c^2$ (Pythagorean theorem).

(2) $\triangle ABC$ is a right triangle.

(3) Therefore, $7^2 + 4^2 = x^2$ (so $x^2 = 49 + 16 = 65$ and $x = \sqrt{65}$).

Of course, you do not usually write all that—you carry out the *modus ponens* without thinking specifically about it.

2. Solve: $3x + 5 = 7$

(1) If $3x + 5 = 7$, then $3x = 2$ (subtract 5 from both sides).

(2) If $3x = 2$, then $x = \frac{2}{3}$ (divide both sides by 3).

(3) Therefore, if $3x + 5 = 7$, then $x = \frac{2}{3}$.

You should recognize this as a transitivity argument. Again, you usually do not write out the *if*'s and *then*'s; you just show the major steps.

$$3x + 5 = 7$$

$$3x = 2$$

$$x = \frac{2}{3}$$

This shows only the premise and the final conclusion. The idea is that $x = \frac{2}{3}$ under the initial condition. Either way you write it, the conclusion follows by a transitivity argument.

3. Prove that BD is the perpendicular bisector of AC if $\triangle ABD$ is congruent to $\triangle CBD$.

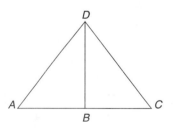

1. $\triangle ABD \cong \triangle CBD$	1. given
2. $AB \cong CB$	2. definition of congruent triangles (apply definition to this triangle by modus ponens)

3. $\angle ABD \cong \angle CBD$	3. definition of congruent triangles again
4. $\angle ABD$ is a right angle	4. supplementary congruent angles are right angles (this principle is applied here by *modus ponens*)
5. BD is the perpendicular bisector of AC	5. definition of perpendicular bisector

The steps shown illustrate the way you would usually write the proof, but notice below how Step 5 was actually accomplished.

BD bisects AC (since $AB \cong BC$).
BD is perpendicular to AC (since $\angle ABD$ is a right angle).
Therefore, BD is the perpendicular bisector of AC.

Look at the conjunctive syllogism above. It bisects *and* it is perpendicular; therefore, it is a perpendicular bisector. You can see that this syllogism is used often—anytime you need to show two things and have to prove them separately. Sometimes the reverse is true and you are given more than you need.

4. Prove that if $ABCD$ is a square, then $\angle A$ is a right angle.

(1) given that a figure $ABCD$ is a square

(2) ($\angle A$, $\angle B$, $\angle C$, $\angle D$ are right angles) *and* ($AB, BC, CD,$ and DA are all congruent)

(3) $\angle A$, $\angle B$, $\angle C$, $\angle D$ are right angles

(4) $\angle A$ is a right angle

Here, Step 2 is a definition of a square but concludes much more than you need. Step 3 uses simplification from Step 2, and Step 4 is another simplification argument from Step 3.

5. Factor $p(x) = x^2 + x + 4$ if possible.

What do you usually do? You try $(x + 4)(x + 1) = x^2 + 5x + 4$ and $(x + 2)(x + 2) = x^2 + 4x + 4$. Since those are the only possibilities, you conclude that $x^2 + x + 4$ does not factor. This is a *modus tollens* argument:

(1) If $p(x)$ factors, then $p(x) = (x + a)(x + b)$ for some integers a and b.

(2) No integers a and b exist (2×2 and 4×1 are the only possibilities; neither works).

(3) Therefore, p(x) cannot be factored.

6. Show that if $\frac{1}{8} > \frac{1}{x}$, then $x \geq 5$ (assume $x > 0$).

1. $\frac{1}{8} > \frac{1}{x}$	1. given
2. $x > 8$	2. multiply both sides by $8x$ (since $x > 0$)
3. $x \geq 5$	3. numbers more than 8 are also more than 5

The last step follows because numbers greater than 8 are no less than 5. Broadening the conclusion with values from 5 to 8 involves an addition argument (*A; therefore, $A \vee B$*). You can view the addition argument this way:

$x > 8$

Therefore, $x > 8$ or $5 \leq x \leq 8$ (i.e., $x \geq 5$).

Basic manipulations of inequalities like this may seem easy, but they are very important in higher math (calculus and up).

Bible—Salvation is an application of a conditional sentence to a person. "Whosoever shall call upon the name of the Lord shall be saved" (Romans 10:13). We often tell a person to put his own name in the verse or to say it in the first person. This *modus ponens* argument applies the conditional principle (if you call, you'll be saved) to the person.

If I call on the name of the Lord, then I shall be saved.
I called on the name of the Lord.
Therefore, I am saved.

A person who understands deductive logic should have less trouble with assurance of salvation. Remember that in valid deductive arguments the conclusion has to be true if the premise is true. Are the premises true? Yes, God cannot lie! In fact, every "whosoever" promise in the Bible, if applied, is a *modus ponens* argument.

Jesus also used deductive logic. The memory verse for this chapter is an example of this.

Memory Verse—Matthew 22:44-45

"The Lord said unto my Lord, Sit thou on my right hand, till I make thine enemies thy footstool? If David then call him Lord, how is he his son?"

The first sentence is quoted from Psalm 110:1. Since David wrote Psalm 110, the word "my" refers to David. "The Lord" is God, the Father (Jehovah); "my Lord" is not the Father since the

Father would not be talking to Himself. The Jews knew that and so they understood that "my Lord" must be David's Savior—or the Messiah as they called Him. They correctly assumed that this Messiah is a man but did not realize that He is more than a man—He is God. The second sentence is a rhetorical question. Jesus asserts that men do not call their children lord. The expected answer then does not argue against His Sonship but shows that He is more than a human son—He is also God. Here is the argument in the form of a syllogism.

1. If David calls Him Lord (the Messiah), then He is not just a son of David.
2. David did call Him "my Lord" in Psalm 110.
3. Therefore, He is not just a son of David.

The *modus ponens* argument is sound. The argument displays perfectly valid deductive logic with true premises. Since the Jews could not refute it, they were baffled. The conditional premise was too obvious to argue (who would worship his own child). The other premise is a clear statement of Scripture. Since the argument was deductive, the reasoning could not be attacked either. Jesus had proved to them that the Messiah is more than just a son of David; He is also God. Since they refused to believe, it is no wonder that they would not ask Him any more questions (Matthew 22:46).

Conclusion

In this chapter you examined the basic deductive arguments. Deductive arguments are classified by validity and soundness. Valid deductive arguments display good reasoning. A sound deductive argument must be valid and must also have true premises. You should know the seven arguments listed in the table on the following page. Remember that each letter can stand for entire Compound statements.

Modus Ponens (MP)

$$A \to B$$
$$\underline{A}$$
$$\therefore B$$

Modus Tollens (MT)
$$A \rightarrow B$$
$$\underline{\sim B}$$
$$\therefore \sim A$$

Disjunctive Syllogism (DS)
$$A \vee B$$
$$\underline{\sim A}$$
$$\therefore B$$

Conjunctive Syllogism (CS)
$$A$$
$$\underline{B}$$
$$\therefore A \wedge B$$

Transitivity Argument (TA)
$$A \rightarrow B$$
$$\underline{B \rightarrow C}$$
$$\therefore A \rightarrow C$$

Simplification Argument (SA)
$$\underline{A \wedge B}$$
$$\therefore A$$

Addition Argument (AA)
$$\underline{A}$$
$$\therefore A \vee B$$

These types can be used in proofs of other argument forms. They can also be used to analyze written arguments, but the arguments must be understood and carefully translated to symbols. Whether you analyze the argument or not, you use these types often. You use them when taking tests, in almost every math problem, and whenever you apply the Bible to your own life. Jesus' own argument proving His deity to the Jews is an excellent model of sound deductive reasoning for you to follow.

Terms

Addition Argument (AA)
Conjunctive Syllogism (CS)
Disjunctive Syllogism (DS)
Modus Ponens (MP)

Modus Tollens (MT)
Simplification Argument (SA)
sound
syllogism
Transitivity Argument (TA)
valid

Questions

1. Use a truth table to prove these forms:
   a. Transitivity Argument
   b. Conjunctive Syllogism
   c. Simplification Argument
2. Prove disjunctive syllogism using a truth table.
3. Prove disjunctive syllogism by the derivation technique.
4. Compare Questions 2 and 3; which was easier? Explain your answer.
5. Symbolize the following argument and then show that it is *not* valid. If a number is not equal to 3, then it is either less than 3 or greater than 3. π is not less than 3 or π is not more than 3. Therefore, π is equal to 3. Which word could be changed to make it valid? Can you prove the argument valid with your change?
6. Symbolize this argument and then show that it is valid by a derivation.

   If either the UN leaders had *not* been satisfied or Iraqi troops had remained in Kuwait, then the Gulf War would not have ended. The war did end. Therefore, it is false to say that if the war ended, then Iraqi troops would have remained in Kuwait.
7. For each argument identify which of the seven types of proof is being attempted. If you can, tell which are valid without doing truth tables or derivations.
   a. People who drink alcohol, later get into hard drugs. Once a person does hard drugs, it is just a matter of time until he dies from an overdose. Thus, drinking alcohol leads to death from a drug overdose.

b. I read a verse that applied to me today. Proverbs 23:17 states, "Let not thine heart envy sinners." I will confess to God my evil desire to be rebellious like Joey.

c. Either own a brand X refrigerator or you will be too embarrassed to have company. We own a brand X refrigerator; therefore, we are not embarrassed when we have company.

d. Waitress! Excuse me, but there are no onions on this pizza. We ordered pepperoni and onions; shouldn't we get both?

e. I must still take logic and calculus. Therefore, I will register for logic.

8. The following arguments refute humanism. For each argument identify it as inductive or deductive and then give the specific type.

a. If humanism is correct, then man is inherently good. Inherent goodness requires loving others; and yet war, deceit, and treachery have been continuously present in the world throughout human history. Thus, humanism must not be correct.

b. Man, like Satan, is proud and rebellious and wants to have things his own way. Thus man is sinful by nature, just like Satan.

c. If the Bible teaches something, then that thing is true. The Bible teaches that man is sinful by nature. Thus, it must be true that man is sinful by nature.

d. Since man has a long history of war with his fellow man and since crime rates and divorce rates continue to escalate, it would appear that man is prone to do evil.

9. Refer to the argument used in the Bible applications based on Romans 10:13. If you are doubting your salvation, then the second premise would be "I am not saved." What *must* the conclusion be using *modus tollens*? (This may also be a help to those struggling with assurance.)

10. Write an essay about Aristotle. Since he was the first great logician, you should write a page or two instead of just a paragraph. What contributions did he make, and how do these contributions relate to this chapter? Draw a conclusion about Aristotle and defend your position.

CHAPTER 8
Complex Inductive Evidence

In Chapter 6 you studied induction techniques. You must understand each type, but in practice people often give more than one reason as evidence for a conclusion. You also evaluate conclusions by testing, questioning, and checking. These activities give rise to very complex discussions. Such intricate arguments frequently come up in science. Theories are offered after organizing many types of information and are then subjected to intense testing. However, you may not realize how often such complex arguments arise outside of science. Theology organizes truth and conclusions drawn from many passages of Scripture. Disagreements cause testing and evaluating. Almost every political comment causes debate because of the complexity of supporting evidence. Each individual has values—especially with regard to how parents should rear children. Your values will be based on complex arguments which include your own childhood experiences and the Scriptures. The principles of this chapter are important because they offer guidelines for evaluating each theory. Using these guidelines, you can evaluate conclusions, not only in science but also in theology and politics. You can also correctly develop and adjust your own values.

Concepts
A **theory** is a conclusion (or a set of interrelated conclusions) drawn from several lines of argument. Because several arguments are involved, the evidence is more complex than with a single argument. In general, most evidence for theories is inductive.

Good theories display seven good qualities or characteristics; these qualities can serve as criteria for identifying good theories.

You can evaluate any theory by testing it against these seven criteria. You can also compare theories to find the best one using these criteria. When even one criterion is not met, it usually (but not always) means that a better explanation exists.

Each good quality is followed by a criterion in question form. The qualities are explained in order of importance, so you should always ask the questions in the order given.

Harmony with Scripture—Is the theory in **harmony with Scripture?** Is it compatible with all Scripture, or are there conflicts? If there is a conflict with the Bible, the theory must be rejected. Although the most important, this test is the one most often overlooked, even by Christians. Are your views (theories) of child rearing, financial management, and entertainment consistent with the Word of God?

Notice that this does not demand that theories of magnetism be based on Scripture. However, the theory must be checked so that it does not contradict Scripture on any point. A theory that contradicts an interpretation of a difficult verse may be suspect, but this suspicion should be distinguished from a clear denial of Scripture. A theory is not automatically wrong just because it contradicts your interpretation of "the spirits in prison" in I Peter 3:19. But a theory that denies that man is sinful is wrong (see Rom. 3:23).

Since the Bible is the only absolutely reliable source of truth, it is really the only source with which a theory must be in complete harmony. This criterion is therefore primary and different in kind from the remaining criteria which follow (see especially *consistency*).

Coherence—Is the theory **coherent?** Does it hang together, or is it self-contradictory? A theory that contradicts itself is its own refutation. If its own tenets cannot be reconciled with one another, it is unreasonable. No one would hire an insane man as a teacher. Why then accept an irrational theory?

Adequacy—Is the theory **adequate** to explain the facts? Does it fit all the data or just some of it? A theory that correctly describes most but not all of the facts is insufficient. The deficiency can be overcome in either of two ways. Perhaps the fact is wrong and when rechecked will be seen to correlate properly with the theory. If rechecking confirms the inexplicable fact, modifications of the theory must be made—by either limiting the data to which the theory can be applied or by extending the theory with additional concepts to account for the observation. A problem at this level is very serious; the theory cannot be left claiming to describe facts that it does not describe.

Consistency—Is the theory **consistent?** Is it in agreement or in conflict with other well-established theories? Since even well-tested theories are not infallible, this is not the same level of inconsistency as conflicts with Scripture. A theory such as relativity that conflicts with Newton's laws of motion is not immediately wrong. It may reveal a limitation to the accepted laws of motion. The inconsistency is clear proof that at least one of the two theories requires modification.

Consistency is not the same as coherency. An incoherent theory contradicts itself; the problem is internal. On the other hand, an inconsistent theory contradicts another theory; the problem is external to both. This is the same way that you describe evidence of witnesses in a court of law. When two legal witnesses contradict each other, they are inconsistent. However, when a single witness contradicts himself, his testimony is incoherent. You would never say that the two witnesses are incoherent with each other. Disagreements of testimony involve lack of consistency. In contrast, when a testimony is incoherent, you can say that it is inconsistent with itself. This text will not use the term inconsistent this way, but the example does show that coherency can be defined as self-consistency.

Simplicity—Is the theory **simple?** Is it efficient or unnecessarily complicated? Inadequate and inconsistent theories often undergo modification, and modifications accumulate as more and more testing is done. Some theories may need to be complicated: complex phenomena may require complex explanations. However, at other times a simple explanation is overlooked because of commitment to an older theory. This happens frequently when you debug a computer program. You patch it and then you patch the patches until the program runs more slowly and eventually ceases to work at all. You should then start from the beginning and rewrite the entire program. There is no virtue in a complicated explanation when a simple one does the same job. Sometimes the truth is too complex to admit a simple explanation. On the other hand, don't accept an unnecessarily complicated theory just because it sounds scholarly. Adequacy at the expense of simplicity is sometimes necessary, but it is not a virtue. The goal is expressed in the maxim "as simple as truthfully possible."

It happens often that simpler, more efficient theories displace those that are overly complicated. Theories generally become more forced and less natural with each modification. **Naturalness** is therefore a synonym for the criterion of simplicity. When the simpler explanation predicts the data that the complex one struggles to account for, it reveals the beauty of the simple, powerful explanation. Thus, the criterion is also called **elegance.** Naturalness and elegance highlight related aspects of the simple theory.

Accuracy—Is the theory **accurate?** Is it precise in explaining the data, or is it approximate? If two theories adequately and simply explain the relevant data, but one is more accurate, the less accurate one must be discarded. You may be surprised that the criterion of accuracy is so low on the list. While accuracy is important, some other things are more so. A theory involving heresy (disharmony with Scripture), insanity (incoherency), or inconsistency cannot be correct no matter how accurate it seems. For instance, Theory A may predict five facts perfectly but cannot account for five others. Theory B explains all ten facts but has a margin of error for all ten. Which is better? Theory B beats Theory A on adequacy even though Theory A happens to generate accurate results in several instances.

Fruitfulness—Is the theory **fruitful?** Is it productive, or is it a dead end? Just like any teaching, theories may be known by their fruits. A theory that suggests no further questions for investigation is a dead end. Again this is less essential than previous criteria. A truly elegant theory is always fruitful even in widely diverse fields of knowledge. The greatest theories have been used in ways that the discoverer never dreamed. Who could have guessed that Riemann's theory of non-Euclidean geometry would be used both for research on the retina of the eye and by Einstein in developing the theory of relativity? An accurate theory should not only predict new results but should also suggest new avenues of research. For this reason, **predictive power** is another name for fruitfulness.

Applications

Science—Copernicus is credited with the heliocentric theory. He proposed that the sun is the center of the solar system. The competing geocentric (or Ptolemaic) theory held that the earth is the center of the solar system. Consider these two views in the diagrams provided.

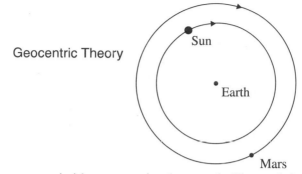

Geocentric Theory

The geocentric idea seems simple enough. The earth is stationary, and all the heavenly bodies revolve around it in circular orbits. But this view faced many difficulties. One difficulty involved the fact that Mars and Jupiter appear to stop and go backwards for a while at regular intervals. A theory of simple circular orbits around Earth cannot adequately account for this backward movement, called retrograde motion. Ptolemy recognized the need for an adequate theory and proposed ''epicycles''—smaller circular orbits centered on the main orbits. Mars orbits on these epicycles while simultaneously orbiting the earth. During half of its epicycle, Mars appears to go backwards. In order to explain fully all the motions of all the planets, the geocentric theory required many epicycles and sometimes even required epicycles on the epicycles.

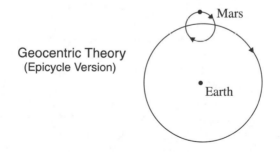

Geocentric Theory
(Epicycle Version)

The modern heliocentric view makes the sun stationary at a focal point of the elliptical orbits of the planets. The backward motion is then explained by the faster speed of the earth as it passes Mars. The difficulties for this view included the lack of experiential evidence of a moving earth, the lack of changes in apparent location of stars, and an apparent conflict with Scripture.

Heliocentric Theory

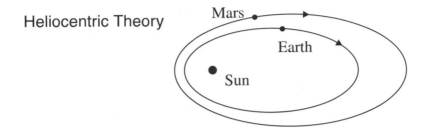

How do these theories compare when you apply the criteria for a good theory? The geocentric view was easily harmonized with Scripture. Man is the highest created physical being (Gen. 1:27), so it was natural to conclude that man's planet was the center of creation. This posed a real problem for the Copernican view. Eventually though, it was realized that the Bible does not say that Earth is the center. The Copernican view was fighting an interpretation of Scripture, not Scripture itself. The struggle to see the harmony was long and bitter, but in the end, neither view conflicts with Scripture.

Both views are coherent. Both views are also adequate. The geocentric view in its original idea was inadequate, but the modifications using epicycles achieved adequacy.

Both views are consistent with known facts; however, the modern theory did not seem consistent. You cannot feel the earth move, and you cannot see stars getting closer as the planet moves. Thus, people considered it a fact that Earth is stationary. Eventually, this "fact" proved to be wrong, though again, the struggle to reconcile experience with the new theory was long. The distances to the stars had to be recalculated to account for the lack of their positional change. Gravity and the size of the earth helped to overcome the problem of not feeling the earth move.

When properly understood, the currently accepted view is much simpler—no epicycles are needed, but simple elliptical orbits are used. The modern view is more accurate, paving the way for the precise prediction of the location of the planet Neptune. It was certainly more fruitful, since it provoked Bible study and scientific research into gravity and star distances. Eventually, the powerful theory permitted the prediction and discovery of comets and new planets, too. The reason for the name Copernican Revolution is now clear. The modern theory had apparent problems at the foundational levels. There seemed to be conflict with Scripture and inconsistency with other accepted laws. Its advantages of simplicity and accuracy were certainly less essential. As the apparent problems were resolved, its predictive power in research aided its acceptance.

Many secular people and liberal Christians claim that Darwin's theory of evolution will displace the creation view in the same way. In reality, though, the Copernican Revolution and the Darwinian Revolution are not analogous. Copernicus challenged a conclusion improperly drawn from Scripture; evolution challenges direct statements of Scripture. Furthermore, geocentrism achieved adequacy at the expense of simplicity. This is the problem with evolution today—not with creation. Those who reject the Bible are not concerned about the conflict with Scripture, so you should be familiar with evolution's weaknesses on the other criteria also. These will be dealt with in the questions at the end of this chapter.

The discovery of penicillin was the result of a fruitful theory. Alexander Fleming hypothesized that a substance must exist to hinder bacterial growth. He discovered lysozyme, which hinders harmless bacteria, but he continued searching, hoping to deter harmful bacteria also. He recognized penicillin when he saw a mold that did not have bacteria growing around it. Most people would have looked at the mold and ignored it. His hypothesis directed his search and caused him to recognize the importance of what he saw.

Similarly, Mendeleev argued by tendency that there was a pattern in the structure of chemical elements. This pattern provided a simple coherent framework for studying the known elements. The vacancies in the pattern displayed an apparent weakness in Mendeleev's theory, unless yet unknown elements could be discovered. The theory prompted fruitful research and soon resulted in the discoveries of gallium, scandium, and germanium. The theory later became the periodic law of the elements.

Bible—You may think that since the Bible is true, you do not need to apply the criteria for testing theories when you study the Scripture. On the contrary, you must apply these criteria all the time. There are two main ways that such criteria must be applied. First, the Bible accurately explains wrong views held by others (such as Satan). When God refutes wrong thinking, you can classify each weakness of the refuted position based on the flaw that God exposed. Classifying the problems associated with each unscriptural view can help you understand what God is telling you. Second, many people tell you what the Bible teaches. Every time you hear a view based on Scripture, these tests can help you decide whether these things are so. Examples for each of these applications follow.

In Acts 14:8-18, Paul and Barnabas were in Lystra trying to refute a false view of God. The Gentiles thought that there were many gods, most having human form, able to do supernatural acts, and acting somewhat pompous (proud to be superhuman). When Paul and Barnabas healed a crippled man, the people of Lystra concluded that they were gods. That was the only adequate explanation they knew for a supernatural act performed by two beings with human form. Paul and Barnabas explained that they were humans, not gods, and that there is only one God (v. 15). This action conflicted with the Gentile view of how gods should act. The people of Lystra had either to modify their theory (to the view that gods could be humble) or to agree that Paul and Barnabas were not gods. This was difficult; if they were not gods, how could they have such power? Paul's explanation struck at the root of their beliefs. Consequently, the people almost rioted and were scarcely restrained from offering sacrifices unto them (vv. 13-18). Of course, the real problem was the conflict between their theory and Scripture. Since people in Lystra did not know any Scripture, they could not evaluate the miraculous events on the most important criterion— God's Word.

Statements in Scripture are also the foundation for the theories of people who study it. Without diligent study and the Holy Spirit's help, some verses may seem contradictory. To theorize on this basis that the Bible contains errors results in a very weak theory. In fact, such a theory is incoherent for Christians. If a person claims to believe the Bible, then he cannot say that there are errors in it. The Bible says concerning itself, "Thy word is truth" (John 17:17). It is self-contradictory to believe in something that claims to be true and at the same time believe there are errors in it. Similarly, some people say Jesus was a great teacher but that He was not God. However, Jesus claimed to be God. It is self-contradictory to say that a man who lies and teaches falsehood is a great teacher. Both of these views must be rejected as incoherent.

Memory Verse—Matthew 22:31-32

"But as touching the resurrection of the dead, have ye not read that which was spoken unto you by God, saying, I am the God of Abraham, and the God of Isaac, and the God of Jacob? God is not the God of the dead, but of the living."

The Sadducees' theory was that the dead are not resurrected (v. 23). This was the basis for the question that they asked Jesus (v. 28). Jesus rebuked them by quoting Exodus 3:6. Since their theology was intended to summarize biblical statements, the quote showed that the theory was not adequate.

Jesus' lesson is masterful, and from His lesson four points can be made. First, He expected them to reason correctly through God's Word ("Have ye not read?" or in other words, "You should know this"). Second, He used a counterexample verse to disprove their generalization. The counterexample can be viewed as a *modus ponens* argument:

If the present tense is used of someone, then that person is alive.

God uses the present tense of Abraham.

Therefore, Abraham is alive.

Since Abraham died long before Moses wrote Exodus 3:6, the only way he could be alive is by resurrection. Third, Christ clearly showed that their theory was inadequate and unscriptural. In fact, Matthew 22:34 states that He silenced them. They could not reply. Fourth, it clearly proves the resurrection, which is one of several fundamental truths of the Christian faith.

What an example! The error of the Sadducees warns you to learn the Scriptures the way Jesus would want you to. Reason carefully in drawing conclusions. Do not settle for an inadequate generalization. Be sure it is founded on the whole counsel of God.

Conclusion

Seven characteristics are required of a good theory: harmony with Scripture, coherency, adequacy, consistency, simplicity, accuracy, and fruitfulness. These principles help not only in the evaluation of scientific thought but also in understanding and drawing conclusions from Scripture (as is expected of us). You also use these ideas in everyday life (see Question 5).

Terms

accurate

adequate

coherent

consistent

elegance

fruitful

harmony with Scripture

naturalness

predictive power

simple

theory

Questions

1. The theory of evolution fails every criterion for a good theory. Each argument against evolution below is based on one criterion. Identify the correct criterion for each.

   a. It contradicts the Second Law of Thermodynamics (that all things run down, decay, become less complex).

   b. Research on the emergence of the first living thing from nonliving substances has had meager results.

   c. Man could not have developed from animals, because it is written, "God formed man of the dust of the ground," (Gen. 2:7).

   d. The simultaneous extinction of so many dinosaurs remains unaccounted for, and also the frozen mammoths have not been explained.

   e. No confirmed "missing links" have been found in over a century of research. Evolutionists have elaborately modified their theory (for example, by hypothesizing beneficial mutations from radiation) to explain this dearth. The creation view naturally supports the lack of transitional forms.

   f. Oldest layers of rock are on the bottom unless there are signs (scrape marks, etc.) of shifting rock layers (strata). The oldest fossils should also be on the bottom. In many parts of the world the topmost strata are considered recent when dated by absence of shifting, but oldest when dated by the fossils in them.

g. How old are the earth and the sun? A creationist can estimate these ages at 7,000 ± 1,000 years. The maximum error is in the thousands of years. Evolutionists typically assign the age of the earth and its error term to the billions of years, and those for the sun to the trillions of years.

Questions 2-4 elaborate arguments in Question 1.

2. Evolutionists struggle to account for the existence of fossils in the "wrong" layer as mentioned in Question 1f. How is the existence of fossils in such layers predicted by creation?

3. Of course, Question 1c is irrelevant to secular evolutionists. Why is Genesis 2:7 better than Genesis 1:27 or Exodus 20:11 to refute theistic evolution?

4. Read *Fossils, Strata and Evolution*, a short pictorial booklet by John G. Read. What fact that is not discussed in Question 1 is virtually impossible for evolutionists to explain?

5. The next examples illustrate the use of theories in daily life. Give the criterion that is not met for each incorrect theory. Assumptions: You and your spouse are happily married. You have a son, Stevie, who can crawl but not speak. You also have a collie which your spouse took to the vet two hours ago. Stevie has a teddy that the collie likes to drag to his bed in the laundry room. Stevie just began to cry and is crawling toward you. It is about noon.

   a. Theory 1: Stevie, being perfect, is weeping for the salvation of souls. (It was a nice attempt to ignore the problem.)

   b. Theory 2: Stevie is hungry. You try to feed him, but he pushes it away. Assuming the statement (theory) that hungry babies eat, what rule of deduction disproves Theory 2?

   c. Theory 3: The dog took his teddy.

   d. Theory 4: The dog took his teddy two hours ago, and Stevie just began to miss it. You find it in the laundry room, but not on the collie's bed. Perhaps the dog did take it. Stevie seems happy to get it. If you think you proved the theory, though, you are committing the fallacy of denying the antecedent (see Chapter 11). Soon Stevie starts to cry again. Teddy only distracted him from his crying.

   e. Theory 5: Stevie had a ten-minute case of malaria (you are getting desperate).

   f. Theory 6: Stevie wanted attention. (This is safe because you cannot test it. In fact, you would have been sure you had the answer until your spouse returned.)

   g. Theory 7: Your spouse greeted Stevie with a big hug and found excellent evidence for _____ .

6. Choose one of the following topics to report on. Include in your report the criterion best illustrated by the discovery and explain how the discovery illustrates it.

   a. Louis Pasteur's theory that "Life comes from life" disproved the theory of spontaneous generation.

   b. Torricelli and Pascal developed the Theory of Atmospheric Pressure which replaced the idea that "Nature abhors a vacuum."

   c. John Couch Adams discovered Neptune. Its existence was theorized and perfectly explained the orbit of Uranus.

   d. Sir Isaac Newton proposed the Theory of Universal Gravitation.

7. Choose a Bible doctrine that you would like to study. Try to choose one that is very controversial today (for example, pretribulationism, separation, immersion, or tongues). List the competing views and analyze the Bible arguments. Which view most adequately accounts for the Bible statements?

8. Treat the Hindu world-view as a theory and show how it fails at least three criteria for a cogent theory.

9. Using the library, find out what Ockham's razor is. How does Ockham's razor relate to the study of inductive arguments?

10. Write a paragraph on William of Ockham (sometimes spelled Occam). Discuss the works that influenced him and his contributions to logic. Also, show how his view of logic was influential in church history.

CHAPTER 9
Hypothetical Deductive Reasoning

In Chapter 8 you studied theories, which are more complex inductive arguments. This chapter focuses on more complex deductive arguments. You will survey methods of proof involving complex deductive arguments. Notice that three principles underlie all of these methods: the law of deduction, the law of cases, and the law of contradiction.

Concepts

The law of deduction—The method of conditional proof is another name for the **law of deduction**, because it is used to prove conditional statements. This technique allows you to assume A, if you desire to prove $A \rightarrow B$. If you succeed in proving B based on your assumption, then A does imply B as desired.

1.	A	1.	assumption for law of deduction
.	.	.	.
.	.	.	.
.	.	.	.
n.	B	n.	Prove B using normal rules.
$n+1$.	$A \rightarrow B$	$n+1$.	law of deduction

One way to see the appropriateness of this method is to consider the truth table for $A \rightarrow B$. Recall that the conditional is always true except when A is true and B is false. If you can eliminate this exception, you will know that the conditional is true. When A is false, the conditional cannot be false. When A and B are both true, the conditional is also true. Thus, you need only show that B cannot be false when A is true. To show this, assume that A is true and prove that B must also be true. This eliminates the exception, so $A \to B$ is true.

You will also recognize the method by showing it this way:

$$\frac{A}{\therefore B}$$

If you can prove B from A, then $A \to B$ is consistent with your method of symbolizing arguments. (In fact, this is where your symbolizing method comes from.)

Usually, you will indent steps 1, . . . , n in law of deduction proofs to show that your temporary assumption is not used anywhere else in the proof unfairly. Of course, you cannot just assume A anywhere you like. Be careful to use the assumption only in the proof of the conditional. These steps cannot be used outside of the indenting.

The law of cases—The **law of cases** contains a simple truth. Either A or $\sim A$ is true. Since $A \vee \sim A$ is always true, it can be used as a step in any proof. Another way to say this is that the following argument form is valid.

$$\frac{\begin{array}{l} A \to B \\ \sim A \to B \end{array}}{\therefore B}$$

No matter what is true of A, B is true. Both the expression $A \vee \sim A$ and the argument form can be proved by truth tables. Since the argument form involves two implications, you can use your previous principle to prove B by cases.

Case 1	1.	A	1.	assumption
	.	.	.	.
	.	.	.	.
	.	.	.	.
	n.	B	n.	proved normally
	$n + 1$.	$A \to B$	$n + 1$.	law of deduction
Case 2	$n + 2$.	$\sim A$	$n + 2$.	assumption
	.	.	.	.
	.	.	.	.
	.	.	.	.
	m.	B	m.	proved normally
	$m + 1$.	$\sim A \to B$	$m + 1$.	law of deduction
	$m + 2$.	B	$m + 2$.	law of cases

Notice that the steps numbered $n + 1$ and $m + 1$ are the premises for the law of cases argument in the last step.

This is used commonly to prove a statement true for all numbers. For instance, to prove that the square of any number is positive, you can prove the result for positive numbers and negative numbers separately and then combine the cases.

Case 1 $x \geq 0$ Since a positive times a positive is positive, $x^2 = x \cdot x \geq 0$.

Case 2 $x < 0$ Since a negative times a negative is positive, $x^2 = x \cdot x \geq 0$.

Therefore, $x^2 \geq 0$.

The law of contradiction—The **law of contradiction** is based on a simple fact: a statement cannot be both true and false. Use a truth table to check that $A \wedge \sim A$ is always false. When $A \wedge \sim A$ occurs as a step in a proof, there must be a false premise somewhere. This constitutes proof that the premise is false. Proofs using this law are called **indirect proofs.** In symbols:

$B \rightarrow R$
$\underline{B \rightarrow \sim R}$
$\therefore \sim B$

You can prove this using truth tables, but the method below is faster. Note that the derivation takes advantage of the law of cases.

1. $B \rightarrow R$	1. given
2. $B \rightarrow \sim R$	2. given
3. $\sim R \rightarrow \sim B$	3. contrapositive rule (Step 1)
4. $R \rightarrow \sim B$	4. contrapositive rule (2)
5. $\sim B$	5. law of cases (3, 4)

Now that you have seen that a contradiction like $A \wedge \sim A$ is impossible, you can see the reasonableness of this idea.

1.	$\sim B$	1.	assumption for law of contradiction
.	.	.	.
.	.	.	.
.	.	.	.
$n.$	A	$n.$	proved normally
.	.	.	.
.	.	.	.
.	.	.	.
$m.$	$\sim A$	$m.$	proved normally
$m + 1.$	$A \wedge \sim A$	$m + 1.$	conjunctive syllogism (n, m)
$m + 2.$	B	$m + 2.$	law of contradiction

The contradiction $A \wedge \sim A$ proves the assumption ($\sim B$) false, and so its negation (B) must be true.

Applications

Logic—The three methods you have just studied are very powerful tools in constructing and evaluating deductive arguments. Analyze the following argument.

> If the national debt increases, the economy will collapse; and if taxes increase, then many mothers will have to neglect their families because they will have to work outside the home. Either the national debt or taxes will increase. Therefore, either the economy will collapse or families will be neglected.

First, symbolize the argument to check for validity. An argument of this form is called a **constructive dilemma**.

$$[(D \rightarrow E) \wedge (T \rightarrow N)]$$
$$\underline{D \vee T}$$
$$\therefore E \vee N$$

You could check this using a truth table (see Chapter 7). The truth table would have 16 rows and 15 columns, so a proof should be easier. Since it seems reasonable that one of the hypotheses should guarantee at least one of the conclusions, you can attempt a derivation. Since $E \vee N$ is not a conditional, the law of deduction is not immediately applicable. You can use either the law of cases or the law of contradiction.

First, study the following example, which proves the argument by cases.

1. $(D \to E) \wedge (T \to N)$		1. given	
2. $D \vee T$		2. given	
3. $D \to E$		3. simplification argument (1)	
4. $T \to N$		4. simplification argument (1)	
	5. D		5. Case 1
	6. E		6. *modus ponens* (3, 5)
	7. $E \vee N$		7. addition argument (6)
	8. $D \to (E \vee N)$		8. law of deduction (5-7)
	9. $\sim D$		9. Case 2
	10. T		10. disjunctive syllogism (2, 9)
	11. N		11. *modus ponens* (4, 11)
	12. $E \vee N$		12. addition argument (11)
	13. $\sim D \to (E \vee N)$		13. law of deduction (9-12)
14. $E \vee N$		14. law of cases (8-13)	

Notice that it can be proved more than one way. Here is another proof of the same statement using the law of contradiction.

1. $(D \to E) \wedge (T \to N)$		1. given	
2. $D \vee T$		2. given	
	3. $\sim(E \vee N)$		3. assume goal false (negated)
	4. $\sim E \wedge \sim N$		4. negation of disjunction (3)
	5. $\sim E$		5. simplification argument (4)
	6. $\sim N$		6. simplification argument (4)
	7. $D \to E$		7. simplification argument (1)
	8. $T \to N$		8. simplification argument (1)
	9. $\sim D$		9. *modus tollens* (5, 7)
	10. $\sim T$		10. modus tollens (6, 8)
	11. T		11. disjunctive syllogism (2, 9)
	12. $T \wedge \sim T$		12. conjunctive syllogism (10, 11)
13. $E \vee N$		13. law of contradiction (3-12)	

Both the law of cases and the law of contradiction prove the validity of the argument. If you disagree with the original argument, you must disagree with a premise—not with the reasoning.

How then can you decide which method to use? The method of direct proof illustrated in Chapter 7 will work for any proof, but may not be the easiest method. Likewise, the law of contradiction always applies—but you must be sure to negate your goal correctly. The other methods of proof may be easier but have other limitations. To apply the law of cases, you must view your possibilities in two classes. The law of deduction will work to prove only conditionals or biconditionals. Knowing which way works fastest comes only with practice, but the following list will help you identify the easiest method.

1. Is the conclusion of the argument a conditional?
    a. Is there a simple transitivity argument?
    b. Can you directly prove the contrapositive?
    c. Can the law of deduction be used?
2. Can you divide it into cases?
3. Try direct reasoning as in Chapter 7.
4. Try to use the law of contradiction. Negate carefully.

What should you do if you need to prove a biconditional statement? Prove the two conditional statements separately, using the law of deduction. The final step combines Steps $n + 1$ and $m + 1$.

1.	A	1.	assumption
.	.	.	.
.	.	.	.
.	.	.	.
$n.$	B	$n.$	derived
$n + 1.$	$A \rightarrow B$	$n + 1.$	law of deduction
$n + 2.$	B	$n + 2.$	assumption
.	.	.	.
.	.	.	.
.	.	.	.
$m.$	A	$m.$	derived
$m + 1.$	$B \rightarrow A$	$m + 1.$	law of deduction
$m + 2.$	$A \leftrightarrow B$	$m + 2.$	definition of biconditional

Finally, how can categorical statements be proved? Each of the four types requires a different method.

Universal Positive:

All A are B. Symbolize it as $A \rightarrow B$. Prove this like other conditional statements.

Universal Negative:

No A are B. Symbolize it as $A \rightarrow \sim B$. Prove this like other conditionals. Notice especially that the contrapositive of the conditional statement, $B \rightarrow \sim A$, may be easier.

Particular Positive:

Some A are B. Prove that there is at least one A that is also a B. The easiest way is to give an example.

Particular Negative:

Some A are not B. Prove that at least one A is not a B. Again, it is easiest if you can just give an example.

Disproving categoricals is done by proving the negation. To disprove all A are B, prove that some A are not B as discussed above (particular negative).

Medicine—All three laws are also used in medicine. Medical research often uses the law of deduction. When researchers administer a certain drug to mice, the blood pressures of the mice drop. The conclusion is that the drug lowers blood pressure. Of course, the conclusion must be based on tendency using many mice, but the basic form of the argument uses the law of deduction.

Mouse takes drug A.

Mouse's blood pressure drops.

Therefore, if a mouse takes drug A, its blood pressure drops.

The law of cases and the law of deduction are illustrated by medical diagnosis. Suppose Joe comes to Dr. Pratt complaining of nausea, vomiting, and diarrhea. Dr. Pratt recognizes these complaints as symptoms of both influenza and food poisoning. Joe has a very extreme case, but Dr. Pratt knows that the lab needs 24 hours to run tests for bacteria in food poisoning cases. Sometimes the cure for one disease can stimulate another, so Dr. Pratt will not take any chances. He begins the lab test and also prescribes intravenous fluids until the lab test is done. The next morning, the lab reports show that there are no signs of food poisoning (bacterial type). Now Dr. Pratt can safely prescribe an antibiotic for the infections resulting from influenza.

Do you see how Dr. Pratt used both laws? To determine the initial treatment, he used the law of cases. For influenza, food poisoning treatment is detrimental, but intravenous fluids will ease Joe's discomfort. For food poisoning, antibiotics used for influenza aggravate the conditions, but intravenous fluids alleviate them. In either case, Dr. Pratt's treatment with intravenous fluids helps Joe.

He also used the law of contradiction to interpret the lab results.

1. Assume Joe has food poisoning.

2. If Joe has food poisoning, the offending bacteria will be found in his digestive system.

3. Bacteria are in his system (*modus ponens*; 1, 2)

4. No bacteria are in his system (lab test).

5. Joe does not have food poisoning (law of contradiction; 3, 4).

The laboratory test was Dr. Pratt's use of the law of contradiction.

You may have noticed that a *modus tollens* argument (Steps 2, 4, and 5) would be shorter. However, it is best to represent Dr. Pratt's work using the law of contradiction because it clearly expresses the hypothesis that Dr. Pratt had when he ordered the test. Dr. Pratt really was using hypothetical reasoning.

Other—The examples from medicine are typical of many areas of investigation. Police investigations are much like the investigation of a doctor. Hypotheses are made and either verified or rejected after testing. The same can be said when a computer programmer tries to debug a program. He narrows the problem into cases, makes tests, and proves some of his guesses wrong. The same method of reasoning is used by auto mechanics when they fix cars. In chemistry, you often need to identify an unknown substance. Here, too, the investigation proceeds along the same lines as Dr. Pratt's unknown disease investigation. You also use proofs by contradiction in geometry. These basic techniques are used in medicine, police work, computer programming, auto mechanics, science, and math.

Bible—Arguments in or about the Scriptures also use these ideas. Paul argues hypothetically for the resurrection in I Corinthians 15.

> If there be no resurrection of the dead, then is Christ not risen: and if Christ be not risen, then is our preaching vain, and your faith is also vain. Yea, and we are found false witnesses of God; because we have testified of God that he raised up Christ: whom he raised not up, if so be that the dead rise not. For if the dead rise not, then is not Christ raised: And if Christ be not raised, your faith is vain; ye are yet in your sins. Then they also which are fallen asleep in Christ are perished. If in this life only we have hope in Christ, we are of all men most miserable. (vv. 13-19)

Notice that verses 13 and 16 both conclude that Christ is not raised. Verses 20-22 assert that Christ is raised (the historical fact was known to them, but Paul gave evidence by analogy for good measure). This contradiction proves false the assumption "there is no resurrection." After further discussion Paul makes that conclusion in his own way: "Death is swallowed up in victory. O death, where is thy sting?" (vv. 54-55). You may summarize the argument by contradiction:

There is no resurrection.	(assume)
Christ is not risen.	(consequence)
Christ is risen.	(fact)
There is a resurrection.	(law of contradiction)

Just like investigations in science, discussions about Bible teaching use these techniques too. However, it is most important to know these methods because the Bible writers themselves used them!

Memory Verse—Acts 17:2

"And Paul, as his manner was, went in unto them, and three sabbath days reasoned with them out of the scriptures."

You have already studied a complex hypothetical argument in I Corinthians 15. This means that good reasoning skills are necessary to understand Scripture. Now you also see that good reasoning skills are necessary to follow the examples set forth in Scripture.

The memory verse explains that Paul reasoned from the Scriptures to convince the Jews of Thessalonica that Jesus is the Christ

(vv. 1-3). Most importantly you should recognize that Paul habitually reasoned out of the Scriptures everywhere he went ("as his manner was"). Further references to Paul's pattern of reasoning include Acts 17:17; 18:4, 19, 28; and 19:8-10.

Paul's life provides a good model of victorious Christian living. Strive to emulate him in the use of reasoning skills.

Conclusion

In this chapter you have seen three laws of deduction. All of them involve hypothetical reasoning (using temporary assumptions).

The Law of Deduction

Assume A.

Derive B.

$\therefore A \rightarrow B$

The Law of Cases

Assume A.

Derive B.

Assume $\sim A$

Derive B.

$\therefore$ Conclude B.

The Law of Contradiction

Assume $\sim A$.

Derive contradiction $(B \wedge \sim B)$

$\therefore A$

These three laws provide the basis for many specific methods of proof.

Prove a biconditional by showing $A \rightarrow B$ and $B \rightarrow A$.

Assume A.

Derive B. $(\therefore A \rightarrow B)$

Assume B.

Derive A. $(\therefore B \rightarrow A)$

$\therefore A \leftrightarrow B$

Proofs of conditionals (least difficult to most difficult)

1. transitivity argument
2. law of deduction
3. contrapositive rule
4. law of deduction to prove contrapositive
5. law of contradiction

Proofs of categoricals

1. All A are B. Prove the conditional $A \to B$ any of the five ways listed previously.
2. No A are B. Prove the conditional $A \to \sim B$ any of the five ways listed previously.
3. Some A are B. Find a specific example. This is the same as disproving (finding a counterexample to) "No A are B."
4. Some A are not B. Find a specific example. This is the same as disproving "All A are B."

Constructive dilemma

The following argument form expands your list of tools.

$$(A \to B) \land (C \to D)$$
$$\underline{A \lor C}$$
$$\therefore B \lor C$$

The three laws are very important. Their power is seen in the number of rules derived from them in logic. They are also regularly used in medicine, law, science, programming, and math. The Bible uses them also, as you saw in I Corinthians 15.

Terms

constructive dilemma

indirect proof

law of cases

law of contradiction

law of deduction

Questions

1. Each proof below uses hypothetical reasoning. Identify the law used in each.

   a. All the Gentiles have sinned (Rom. 1) and all the Jews have sinned (Rom. 2—especially vv. 17-29). Therefore, all people have sinned (Rom. 3:9-11).

   b. For purposes of argument, suppose that New Age philosophy is correct. If it is correct, then man can overcome his sin problem and evolve into a new species: New Age Man. This will be done by meditation, drugs, positive mental attitude, and other means of self help. There will be peace, equity, and financial security for all. This condition is impossible. History reveals the impossibility of permanent peace. The Bible also asserts that man cannot help himself (John 15:5), that man does not evolve (Romans 8:22), that Christ alone can transform man's thinking (Col. 2:3), and that the poor are always with us (Matt. 26:11). The New Age philosophy is not correct.

   c. All American presidents have moderate views. Why? A liberal candidate will not receive support from conservative voters unless he has some conservative positions. If some of his views are conservative, then he is a moderate liberal. On the other hand, a conservative candidate will not get enough support unless his platform includes some liberal ideas. Both liberal and moderate conservative voters would be alarmed at a staunch conservative candidate, and so, if some of a conservative's views are liberal, he is at most a moderate conservative.

2. Which law is used in making each valid conclusion about Gnosticism?

   a. The Gnostics assume that matter is evil and spirit is good. Since bodies are matter, they must be evil. Since human spirits are housed in bodies, the good spirits are imprisoned in evil bodies. At death, the spirits are released from the prison and become free. Therefore, if matter is evil, death is freedom from evil.

   b. In the Gnostic view (as in part a), no one has a body in heaven. If you did have a body, then the good spirit would be locked again in an evil body, and this is not consistent with any concept of a good heaven. Therefore, in the Gnostic view there is no resurrection.

3. Give counterexamples for each Gnostic generalization. Can you support your counterexamples from Scripture?

a. Matter is evil.

b. Spirit is good.

c. There is no resurrection.

4. Supply reasons for each step in the proof of the **destructive dilemma** below:

1. $(A \rightarrow B) \wedge (C \rightarrow D)$	1. premise
2. $\sim B \vee \sim D$	2. premise
3. $\sim(B \wedge D)$	3. _____
4. $A \wedge C$	4. _____
5. $A \rightarrow B$	5. _____
6. $C \rightarrow D$	6. _____
7. A	7. _____
8. C	8. _____
9. B	9. _____
10. D	10. _____
11. $B \wedge D$	11. _____
12. $\sim(A \wedge C)$	12. _____
13. $\sim A \vee \sim C$	13. _____

5. Show that $A \vee \sim A$ is always true using a truth table.

6. Show that $A \wedge \sim A$ is always false using a truth table.

7. Prove the following argument using the three methods indicated; then identify the easiest method.

a. directly as in Chapter 7

b. using the law of deduction

c. using the law of contradiction

$$A \rightarrow C$$
$$B \rightarrow C$$
$$\overline{(A \vee B) \rightarrow C}$$

8. Make truth tables for the argument forms.
   a. $A \rightarrow B$
      $$\underline{\sim A \rightarrow B}$$
      B

   b. $A \rightarrow B$
      $$\underline{A \rightarrow \sim B}$$
      $\sim A$

9. Research a drug used to treat a disease or ailment. How was the drug discovered? Identify the type of reasoning used in its discovery. What disease(s) does it treat? How is one of these diseases diagnosed? Identify the type of reasoning used in the diagnosis.

10. Write a paragraph on Gottfried Wilhelm von Leibniz, mentioning his contributions to logic.

CHAPTER 10

Fallacies of Induction

You have now completed the basics of good reasoning. In this chapter and the next, you will learn of common mistakes made in reasoning. Classifying errors in reasoning will help you detect faulty reasoning and improve your own reasoning skills. The questions at the end of the chapter will give you practice distinguishing the types of mistakes. This chapter emphasizes mistakes of induction, whereas the next chapter focuses on fallacies in deduction.

Concepts

Mistakes in inductive arguments typically fall into three broad categories. The first involves misuses of proper methods that were discussed earlier, such as an argument from tendency based on an unrepresentative collection of facts. The second includes arguments based primarily on emotion. (A person's reasoning is not necessarily wrong just because you call him a jerk or a dummy.) The third category involves the twisting of evidence, such as taking Bible verses out of context. A mistake in reasoning is called a **fallacy.** Study the fallacies in these three categories of fallacies in more detail.

Weak Induction—Misuse of any of the six inductive techniques results in weak arguments. Chapter 5 warned you against these mistakes, but you should review them here.

In an appeal to authority, the case is weakened if it is based on an **unqualified authority.** The idea of quoting an authority is that he is a respected, knowledgeable, and unbiased expert on the subject under discussion.

False cause is the fallacy in weak appeals to utility. An argument that incorrectly concludes that one event is the cause of another commits the fallacy of false cause. There are three ways that this fallacy can occur. First, you may notice that event *A* often precedes event *B* and conclude that *A* causes *B*. Smoking and lung cancer are properly related this way. However, you always park the car before you enter a store. Does parking cause you to enter the store? No! Both of these actions are caused by your intent to shop at the store. It was your desire to go to the store that caused you to drive there and park to begin with. The false cause based on precedence is termed ***post hoc ergo propter hoc,*** which is Latin for "after this, therefore, because of this." Second, a relationship may be noticed with no time element. A certain microscopic organism is found in every patient with a rare disease. Researchers conclude that the microorganism causes the disease. If this organism is found in healthy people also, then the researchers must look for another cause. The false cause based on relationship is termed ***non causa pro causa,*** which in Latin means "not the cause for the cause." Third, it is possible to chain causes together (of either type). This usually results in a **slippery slope** fallacy. Drinking can lead to use of marijuana. Marijuana use can lead to harder drugs. Harder drugs can lead to heroin. Therefore, people should not drink because they may end up on heroin. There are plenty of good arguments against drinking, but this is *not* one of them. Teens usually recognize slippery slopes and give the "Here we go again" look when a parent uses such reasoning. Parents may commit this fallacy, but they usually have legitimate unstated concerns that wise teens will honor. You can see that these mistakes are common in appeals to tendency. However, please notice that it is the primary mistake in weak appeals to utility. When a patient gets well after receiving a drug, you may believe the drug cured him, but he may have healed in time even without the drug. The fact that something works is not proof of cause.

The common problem with a weak appeal to experience is the **exceptional experience.** Arguments from experience are often used to justify what is normal. Jane may be telling her friend Kate that Mr. Johnson is an easy teacher. She may support this claim with the comment "I got an A in his history class." If this was an exceptional experience, then the argument is weak. If Jane finds history easy or enjoyable, her experience does not prove her point. Perhaps she knows more about history from previous courses or perhaps she was the teacher's pet. Each of these possibilities suggests that her experience may be exceptional and not evidence that Mr. Johnson is easy. For the argument to be strong, Kate must know that Jane performed better in Mr. Johnson's class than in other teachers' history classes at the same level of difficulty and with the same amount of effort. It will also help if Kate's grades are about the same as Jane's.

A weak argument from silence is called an **appeal to ignorance.** In order for you to distinguish, you must think about which position has the "burden of proof." In a sense, you are testing the theory based on which claim *predicts* silence. For this view the appeal to silence may be strong evidence, since the tendency verifies the prediction. One of the clearest examples is in the evolution debate. Creation predicts that there will be no intermediate forms (missing links) found between the species. In over 100 years no clear ones have been found. This argument from silence is strong evidence for creation. On the other hand, some evolutionists claim that though none have been found, some may yet be found. They argue that no one can show that evidence will never be found. This claims a silence of contrary evidence and that the lack of such evidence supports their view. Do you see how this weak appeal has shifted the burden of proof? The creationist view predicts no transitional forms and notes that evolutionists have tried in vain for centuries to find one, but to no avail. Evolution predicts hundreds of transitional forms but ignores the lack of evidence and appeals to possible future evidence. Thus they support the theory of evolution with a theory that there will be evidence. Potential future knowledge does not support any position. Would you advocate the view that humans can fly like Superman, and someday they may remember how? Do not ignore the importance of negative evidence and be sure to discern the burden of proof.

A weak argument by analogy is a **strained analogy.** There are two ways to strain an analogy. The most common strained analogy occurs when two things are compared that are not really comparable. It can also occur when a reasonable analogy is made, but too many points of comparison are argued. In this case the strain comes from **pressing the analogy** too far. Most analogies convey one main point. Only the one intended aspect of comparison should be discussed. Be careful that the resemblance is more than superficial *and* that you argue one point only.

The typical error in arguments from tendency is the **hasty generalization.** In a hasty generalization, a conclusion is drawn that is based on unrepresentative or too limited information. This is the usual weakness in appeals to tendency. When you hear someone complain that the speaker is "jumping to conclusions," the complainer is usually drawing attention to this fallacy.

Emotional Appeals—Appeals to emotions are not proper in argument. It is never right to play upon the emotions of the listener to obtain his consent. This does not mean that emotions are wrong. Emotions must be used in speaking. A good speaker both displays and evokes emotions; when he does not, the speech is flat, dead, and boring. The point here is that the emotions should *follow* the reasons. Solid evidence should be given; then emotional illustrations may be used to drive the point home or motivate people to action. Emotions may illustrate, motivate, or aid recall, but they must not be substituted for evidence. The fallacies below are fallacies because the only evidence offered appeals to an emotion. Six emotional ploys will be discussed here: fear, pity, envy, greed, pride, and hate.

An **appeal to force** is a threat which instills fear. Physical threats come immediately to mind, but threats can include revoked privileges (as every child knows). Threats never prove the point. Even if the person obeys, he may not be convinced in his own mind. The speaker attempts to manipulate the hearers through fear.

An **appeal to pity** is a tear-jerking story intended to provoke sympathy and a response. Such a story should not be used as a reason for financial support, although it may rightly motivate support if good reasons have already been given. A picture of a poor starving child in Burma is not a reason to support a specific missionary to Burma. Slides of poor people do not prove that the missionary will help the poor. Slides of the missionary distributing food, witnessing, and preaching are more relevant. The appeal to pity does not indicate either the compassion or faithful service of the missionary. Humanists can use emotional manipulation just as well as a good missionary. Be sure your dollars go to proper Christian work, and do not succumb to deception under the cloak of compassion.

An **appeal to vanity** causes envy, making you feel as if you are truly missing out on something that someone else has. The appeal manipulates you through jealousy or covetousness. The advertising industry is a master of this deception. Ads make you want to be like the person shown who is attractive, smart, athletic, or highly skilled. Such reasoning is clearly wrong. In fact, it is sin to be controlled by envy. After listing envyings among the works of the flesh, God says, "they which do such things shall not inherit the kingdom of God" (Gal. 5:21).

An **appeal to the purse** plays upon greed, making you want more than you have. The arguer seeks to manipulate the hearer through his desire for selfish gain. "The love of money is the root of all evil" (I Tim. 6:10). Thus, personal pleasure, rather than jealousy of others, distinguishes this fallacy from the appeal to vanity. Resist greed: "Be content with such things as ye have" (Heb. 13:5).

An **appeal to the people** manipulates feelings of pride. Political leaders rouse your love for a nation, state, city, or political party. However, this appeal is not limited to politics. Your emotions may be stirred for your alma mater, business, religious denomination, or any other group you identify with. While some of your decisions may be right, this kind of appeal is not the right reason for the decision. "Pride goeth before destruction" (Prov. 16:18).

An **argument against the person** encourages feelings of hate or enmity. Here it is not the person's viewpoint that is attacked, but the person himself. Two varieties are typical. Verbal abuse may be heaped upon the person. The speaker may call him all kinds of malicious names. The second variety undermines his reputation by recounting stories showing questionable behavior or circumstances. This is commonly called character assassination. It is very important to recognize that this is a fallacy even if it is completely true. If the accusation is false, it is slander. If the accusation is true, it still does not refute the accused person's position. Imagine that Mr. Slick is a very wicked politician. He is an atheist and promotes humanism and evolution and will do anything to achieve his objective. He also takes a very liberal stand on welfare, but he opposes abortion. Some people attack Mr. Slick's views on welfare because he is a "godless humanist." Indeed, he is a godless humanist, but that is just as irrelevant to his views on welfare as it is to his views on abortion. Is abortion right because Mr. Slick opposes it? It is very important to argue the issues and not the people who hold them. Many fallacies have Latin names; the Latin name for this one, *ad hominem,* is frequently used.

Twisted Evidence—This third class of fallacies is intermediate between the other two. The emotional appeals above provide no solid evidence since it neither selects nor applies a proper method of induction. The weak inductions discussed earlier select a correct method but fail to apply the method correctly. These errors offer no solid evidence (like the emotional appeals), but at first glance they appear to use a correct method (like the weak inductions). The apparently correct form is superficial, so these can be tricky. These four fallacies are also often confused with each other, so consider them very carefully.

The fallacy of **suppressed evidence** is made when pertinent information is not presented. The conclusions drawn from the relevant material presented are correct. But the conclusions would appear weaker if the whole truth were told. The fallacy is classified this way even when evidence is withheld unintentionally. Remember that, in this case, the written argument appears strong, but only part of the truth is told. Unless you can state facts to the contrary that have been withheld or overlooked, you should not classify the argument as suppressed evidence.

Missing the point is the fallacy committed when the strong conclusion is ignored and an alternate is substituted. In contrast to suppressed evidence, the flaw lies not in the evidence or premises but in the conclusion. If you can supply the correct point, you know that the argument commits this fallacy.

You commit the fallacy of the **straw man** when you oversimplify an opponent's argument before refuting it. It is easy to demolish the straw, but it is not fair to consider the real view refuted. It is often necessary to paraphrase. You cannot respond to an editorial without referring to the stated position. If you represent the position fairly, there is no fallacy. Giving your rebuttal to the paraphrase is not the problem either. The error occurs when you substitute an inaccurate paraphrase (a new set of premises) for the original. When people say, ''Quit putting words in my mouth,'' they are complaining that you are perpetrating this fallacy on them. Since the problem is with the new premises, it is not missing the point (problem in conclusion only). It is not suppressed evidence since the premises are replaced and are not just incomplete. The misrepresented position, being characteristic of a rebuttal in progress, is most helpful in identifying the fallacy.

When a person commits the **red herring** fallacy, you might say that he ''changed the subject'' or ''went on a rabbit trail.'' Be careful, though. In suppressed evidence the subject was distorted but not changed. When an argument misses the point, the conclusion may be on the subject but incorrect. In the straw man, the paraphrase has changed the viewpoint but not the subject. It should be clear that the first three fallacies are easy to confuse with this one. Notice that there were clear signs for the first three. The safest plan of classification is to look for the others first. If there is some change of subject and the argument does not fit the other three descriptions, it should be safe to classify it here.

Finally, remember that strong arguments may still be uncogent. This is the case when no fallacy is committed, but a false premise occurs. The term fallacy refers to errors in reasoning, not to false statements. A false statement is not a fallacy, although the word *fallacy* is used loosely in that sense. (Loose usage: "George Washington was a Communist." "No, he wasn't; that's a fallacy.") Every weak argument contains a fallacy and is uncogent. A strong argument is uncogent if it contains a false premise. Of course arguments may have both a false premise and a fallacy and so be uncogent for two reasons (but weak for just one reason).

Applications

Business—Advertising is full of fallacies. Are the fallacies there because the business thinks they are good arguments? No. The business has not made a mistake; the fallacies are there on purpose. The business knows that emotional appeals generate more sales. They are not interested in whether they state half-truths (as long as they cannot be sued); the main point is sales. This kind of advertising is *not* right for a Christian businessman. The Bible requires honesty. If you evaluate commercials logically, you will build sales resistance and be a better steward of God's money. Study these examples of advertisements for Sparkle toothpaste.

Weak Induction

1. *Unqualified authority*: An excellent juggler is juggling five flaming and sparkling torches. His smile gives a sparkle and he says, "Sparkle is the best." (Is the juggler a dentist?)

2. *False cause*: Tough guy winks at beautiful gal. Both smile and their teeth sparkle. As they depart arm in arm, the title reads, "Sparkle for a sparkling evening." (He got the date, but was the toothpaste responsible?)

3. *Exceptional experience*: A man gives personal testimony of cured dental problems within a month after trying Sparkle. His dentist confirms the testimony. (Is this case representative?)

4. *Appeal to ignorance*: An average looking man at a restaurant asks his nice looking waitress for a date. She starts to hedge, "Well, . . . um . . ." He smiles and his teeth sparkle, then she accepts. Title reads, "Sparkle. You can never know what might make a difference." (Perhaps, but which side has the burden of proof?)

5. *Strained analogy*: A hiker relaxes under a pine by a glacial lake with snowy peaks *sparkling* in the background and reflecting in the lake. "Sparkle's new flavor will remind you of a sparkling day in the mountains. Like the mountains it will bring peace." (Any such resemblance is superficial.)

6. *Hasty generalization*: Thirty of forty dentists surveyed in Beverly Hills recommended Sparkle. "Use Sparkle, the dentist's choice." (Dentists in one city may not be representative of all dentists nationwide.)

Emotional Appeals:

7. *Appeal to force*: "If you won't use Sparkle, we'll just have to call you 'Gloomy.' " (Oh no!)

8. *Appeal to pity:* "Buy Sparkle toothpaste. We may not be number 1, but we're trying." (Aw! Poor Sparkle.)

9. *Appeal to vanity*: A nice looking man whispers sweet nothings in a woman's ear, while a waiter brings flaming skewers toward their table in the background. "Sparkle keeps you ready for those close times." (Does it make you want to use Sparkle so you can be young, good looking, and romantic?)

10. *Appeal to the purse*: "Buy Sparkle and save!" (But which brand is better?)

11. *Appeal to the people*: A parade scene shows U.S. flags and a band playing the national anthem. U.S. troops follow, led by a car carrying the smiling general. The general's teeth sparkle as he says, "Sparkle . . . America's toothpaste." (How many brands are made in the U.S. anyway?)

12. *Argument against the person:* "Buy Sparkle. Crust is just a flavored gel pushed by rich business tycoons who are only

out for a buck. Don't get Crust—get Sparkle.'' (Badmouthing the competition does not undercut their product nor prove that another product is better.)

Twisted Evidence

13. *Suppressed evidence*: ''This year, for the third time in five years, the annual survey of dentists identified Sparkle as the most recommended toothpaste.'' (What about the other two surveys?)

14. *Missing the point*: ''Although Sparkle is relatively new on the market, it is certainly better than Crust. More Crust users have cavities than Sparkle users.'' (The first sentence admits that Crust has more sales, so of course more cavities are found. Compare percentages not raw data. It is like saying more people die in car accidents than in climbing Himalayan peaks. Therefore, is driving riskier than climbing Himalayan peaks?)

15. *Straw man*: ''We asked an executive for Crust to comment on the new competition from Sparkle. He said he was busy. He obviously considers Sparkle too insignificant to waste his time on. Such an obnoxious attitude should be treated in kind. Why waste your time with Crust? Buy Sparkle.'' (Does the third statement interpret the Crust representative fairly?)

16. *Red herring*: ''Sparkle is the best toothpaste for reducing cavities. Our survey of 1,000 dentists showed that cavities are America's number one dental problem.'' (I thought you were trying to show that Sparkle fights cavities; what do those dentists say about that?)

These fallacies occur in many contexts besides advertising. Others will be considered in the questions.

Bible—Read Acts 19:23-41. The silversmith Demetrius incited a riot by using the fallacy of the appeal to the people. He stirred up the other silversmiths first through pride concerning their trade. Then this group stirred up the people of Ephesus through pride in the reputation of the city as the main center for worship of their goddess Diana. Emotions ran high, and they arrested two of Paul's companions (v. 29). The mob chanted for hours (v. 28, and then two more hours in v. 34). These mob reactions are dangerous; the disciples were wise in restraining Paul (v. 30).

Alexander was shouted down (vv. 33-34); Paul may have been killed! Finally, the town clerk, one of their own, was able to speak some reason and deflate the fallacy that began the riot. He pointed out that the men had not taken any action against Diana or Ephesus. (Paul tactfully preached the truth without attacking error. Demetrius correctly recognized the conclusion that if Christ was the only God, Diana was false—but apparently Paul had not attacked Diana in so many words, v. 37.) The town clerk also said that if they knew Diana was great, they should not need to shout it (v. 36).

This account shows the extreme danger of these fallacies. The emotional appeals of Demetrius racked the whole city and came close to creating a lynch mob.

Memory Verse—II Peter 3:3-6

"Knowing this first, that there shall come in the last days scoffers, walking after their own lusts, and saying, Where is the promise of his coming? for since the fathers fell asleep, all things continue as they were from the beginning of the creation. For this they willingly are ignorant of, that by the word of God the heavens were of old, and the earth standing out of the water and in the water: Whereby the world that then was, being overflowed with water, perished."

This is an amazing refutation of evolution. In modern times, people say that things continue as they always have—gradually. They reject the possibility of miracles and Jesus Christ's return. In fact, Peter paraphrases their view fairly. There are no miracles *since* things continue gradually. This argument is an argument based on tendency. The natural world is predictable. You can observe seasonal patterns of erosion this year and find the same pattern ten years later. The argument for this gradual pattern is not based solely on one person's experience—everyone sees the same pattern. It is a hasty generalization, though, because the patterns noticed in the last few hundred years may not have been consistent for all time. In fact, the observations of an evolutionist who believes in millions of years form a very, very small sample to base a case on.

Peter pointed out the fallacy. They are willingly ignorant that God created the world (rising out of water and still surrounded by water—see Genesis 1:6-10), and destroyed it with a flood (using both water sources—see Genesis 7:11-12). These events were not gradual; they provide counterexamples to the generalization, showing its error. How can you know God did these things? The argument is based on authority—the Word of God. God knows what He did; He was there, and He told us. His is the only eye-witness experience of creation.

If you continue beyond verse 6 (II Peter 3:7-12), you see that Peter says (vv. 7, 10, 12) that God will destroy the world again in judgment. This time the world will melt—and this event will not be gradual either.

He goes on to argue that man cannot judge God by man's own ideas of fast and slow. Life is short, but God is eternal. A day for God is *like* a thousand years for man. God is showing His love for more people to be saved (vv. 8-9). Some people use verse 8 to say that the days of creation could have been thousands of years each—long enough for evolution. This conclusion is impossible on two counts. First, the verse has been lifted out of context and used to support the very idea that the context condemns. Second, the verse does not say one day is "a thousand years" but "*as* a thousand years." Using verse 8 that way commits the fallacy of suppressed evidence (ignoring the rest of the passage and even the specifics in the passage to make a point).

Finally, Peter says that this argument should influence the way you live (v. 11), giving hope and purpose for life (v. 13). Peter was a fisherman. He did not have the advantage of the thorough academic background that Paul had, but he did use what he had well enough to test principles against the Scriptures, and he could spot false teaching when he saw it. It is important to know the common fallacies. Even if you forget the names of the fallacies, you should recognize when an argument is weak. This will help you to prove (test) all things (I Thess. 5:21, II John 9-10, I John 4:1).

Conclusion

Fallacies are weaknesses in reasoning, and false premises are not included. The following sixteen fallacies were grouped into three broad classes of inductive fallacies: weak induction, emotional appeal, and twisted evidence. A brief description of each fallacy is given (with its Latin name, if it has one).

Weak Induction

1. unqualified authority   weak appeal to authority
                            (argumentum ad verecundiam)
2. false cause   weak appeal to utility
3. exceptional experience   weak appeal to experience

4.	appeal to ignorance	weak appeal to silence *(argumentum ad ignorantiam)*
5.	strained analogy	weak appeal to analogy
6.	hasty generalizations	weak appeal to tendency

Emotional Appeal

1.	appeal to force	plays on fear *(ad baculum)*
2.	appeal to pity	plays on pity *(ad misericordiam)*
3.	appeal to vanity	plays on envy *(ad invidiam)*
4.	appeal to the purse	plays on greed *(ad crumenam)*
5.	appeal to the people	plays on pride *(ad populum)*
6.	argument against the person	plays on hate *(ad hominem)*

Twisted Evidence

1.	suppressed evidence	presents partial truth
2.	missing the point	changes conclusion *(ignoratio elenchi)*
3.	straw man	changes opponent's position
4.	red herring	changes topic

An understanding of these fallacies sheds light on advertising techniques and helps you avoid being misled into buying poor products. Knowledge of these fallacies can also help you in "rightly dividing the word of truth" (II Tim. 2:15). You can recognize when people twist Scripture and understand rebuttals recorded in Scripture, as when Peter refuted the scoffers.

Terms

appeal to ignorance

appeal to force

appeal to pity

appeal to the people

appeal to the purse

appeal to vanity

argument against the person

emotional appeal

exceptional experience

fallacy

false cause
hasty generalization
missing the point
red herring
strained analogy
straw man
suppressed evidence
twisted evidence
unqualified authority
weak induction

Questions

1. Match the types of inductive arguments.

1.	strong and cogent	A.	impossible
2.	weak and cogent	B.	fallacy
3.	strong and uncogent	C.	good argument
4.	weak and uncogent	D.	false premise

2. Find two newspaper or magazine advertisements that play on the emotions. Identify the specific emotional appeal in each.

3. Find an editorial that twists evidence. Identify which type of twisting is used.

4. Find an advertisement that misuses a proper method of inductive argument and identify the misuse.

5. Identify each fallacy in the following areas of politics, psychology, business, etc.

   a. You tell me that I need to accept the gospel and be saved from my sins, but you can't tell me I'll be saved from my sins when you admit that you still commit evil deeds.

   b. Yes, I know Joey has that bad habit, but he can't help it. You know those phlegmatic personality types.

   c. The neighbor's three children could not read before they went to school. My child was able to read before school. Therefore, three out of four children cannot read before they go to school.

   d. Last year there was a 2 percent increase in our costs. In spite of that, our company's profits increased 4 percent.

Next year we face an 8 percent cost increase. Since our profits increased twice as much as our costs last year, we should increase profits 16 percent this year.

e. Potato prices increased 3 percent this year. Carrots went up 4 percent, peas up 3 percent, and corn up 5 percent. How can anyone survive? These vegetables alone represent a combined total of a 15 percent increase and the cost-of-living raise was only 4 percent.

f. On the Revised Stanford-Binet Test for IQ, Billy got a 92 and Jesse got a 95. Therefore, according to the test, Jesse is smarter than Bill.

6. Fallacies of misused inductions. Match each argument to the main fallacy committed.

A. appeal to authority

D. false cause

B. appeal to ignorance

E. exceptional experience

C. hasty generalization

F. strained analogy

1. I brought my umbrella so it would not rain; it never rains when I bring it.

2. Eventually life on other planets will be found. No one yet has shown that this is impossible.

3. I will never buy another Ford; my last one had a dozen breakdowns in the first year.

4. Dad, can I use the car? Mom said I could.

5. Everyone I know is going to vote for Larson. Larson will win the election.

7. Each argument below involves a fallacy of emotion or a fallacy of twisted evidence. Identify the basic fallacy employed.

A. suppressed evidence

F. appeal to pity

B. against the person

G. red herring

C. appeal to force

H. appeal to vanity

D. missing the point

I. straw man

E. appeal to the people

J. appeal to the purse

1. Suicide is wrong because it is murder. Murder is illegal and against the Bible; laws must be enforced for human safety.

2. Abortion should be legal since statistics show that many of the children would be unwanted babies of single parents.
3. Be the first on your block to get this new robot duster.
4. J. Fenton supports welfare. I always knew he was a lazy bum anyway.
5. J. Fenton supports welfare. Since welfare encourages laziness, Fenton is seeking for bums to be supported by the responsible workers. We must oppose Fenton's program.

8. Some of the following arguments contain fallacies. Others do not. For each inductive argument, identify it as strong or weak. If strong, give the technique used. If weak, give the fallacy committed.

   a. I know I shouldn't let Johnny get away with deceiving me, but I can't bear to spank him. God gave me the gift of mercy, you know.
   b. Three different rats each ate one of those pills, and all died within four hours. Those pills must be lethal to rats.
   c. A year ago we had to implement a 20 percent pay cut, as you all know. This year we are implementing a 20 percent pay raise to restore the original salaries.
   d. Acts 4:12 says that ''there is none other name [besides Jesus] under heaven given among men whereby we must be saved.'' On this basis we can say that Buddhists are not saved.
   c. I know God is guiding me because yesterday I met Him face to face and He said, ''I am Alpha and Omega. Go to Albania as a missionary!''
   f. For your own best interest, you should stop submitting sloppy and incomplete work. You will be without a job otherwise.
   g. Perhaps you were not aware that the seminar topics were my suggestions. If you continue to suggest topics, I will be forced to terminate you, Miss Parks.
   h. It is not important whether you choose a secular or Christian school. Daniel was given secular schooling. The important thing is that you study hard. Proverbs 13:4 commands diligence.

    i. I know that God would not want me to participate in that activity, because I did it too much before I was saved and my conscience hurts me now when I think about it.

    j. In Revelation 2–3 there are letters to seven churches in Asia. Some interpreters think these are symbolic of periods in church history. This is impossible because the view originated with amillennialists.

9. Explain why emotional appeals are not classified with weak inductions or twisting evidence.

10. Write a paragraph on John Stuart Mill. Discuss his contributions to causation arguments. Which two fallacies would be clearly exposed by his work?

CHAPTER 11
Fallacies of Deduction

In the last chapter you learned that a **fallacy** is an error in the reasoning (not the truth value of the premises). You surveyed three classes of errors in inductive reasoning. This chapter introduces errors in deductive reasoning.

Concepts

Of course, some deductive arguments have false premises. This makes the deduction unsound, but not necessarily invalid. A very common example of this is a **false dichotomy**. The premise is false because it contains a disjunction that claims that there are only two possibilities when there are really more. "Either believe in evolution or be unscientific" is one such example. A disjunctive syllogism using the above premise may be valid, though unsound:

> He believes in evolution or he is unscientific.
> Pete does not believe in evolution.
> Therefore, Pete is unscientific.

No one disagrees with the reasoning—the syllogism is valid and no fallacy is committed. The argument is unsound because of the false premise, in this case a false dichotomy.

Invalid deductive arguments fall into two groups: formal fallacies and informal fallacies. **Formal fallacies** are those argument forms that do not check when a truth table is made. There is a clear-cut error that becomes visible in symbolic form. **Informal fallacies** are more subtle. In these, the error is not in the truth value of a statement (as in false dichotomy), nor in the symbolic form (formal fallacy), but in the relationship between the statements; such errors are recognized only by examining context.

Informal Fallacies—There are five common mistakes related to context.

Equivocation involves changing the meaning of a term. A clear example of this follows.

> All animals having trunks are elephants.
> Snoopy has a trunk (when he goes on vacation).
> Therefore, Snoopy is an elephant (when he goes on vacation).

This argument follows *modus ponens*.

$$T \rightarrow E$$
$$\underline{T}$$
$$\therefore E$$

The problem is that *trunk* has changed meaning from ''proboscis'' to ''suitcase.'' Each meaning is clear in context, but the relationship of the premises falls apart since the symbol T is only superficially the same in both premises.

Accident is the application of a principle to a situation that it was not intended to cover.

> All men are sinners.
> Jesus is a man.
> Therefore, Jesus is a sinner.

This argument is a simple *modus ponens;* the problem here is that the universal (all men) is intended to mean ''all simple humans'' or ''all humans that are not also God.'' The intended meaning of the premise is misapplied to an exceptional case. Thus again, the premises are improperly related. This is the reverse problem of hasty generalization—you might call it a hasty application.

Composition improperly draws a conclusion about an entire whole based on the parts.

> All humans are sinful.
> Humanity is the set of humans.
> Therefore, humanity is sinful.

Again, the argument has correct form for *modus ponens*. The fault is in content. The quality of being human is not in itself sinful. God did not create sin. Adam was human and was created good. Christ was human and was good. You cannot reason from the sinful state of each living man to the sinfulness of the whole race as a race.

Division is the reverse of composition. A truth about a whole is improperly attributed to a part.

> All humans are sinful.
> Your body is human.
> Therefore, your body is sinful.

Again, the form of argument (*modus ponens*) is valid. Once again, though, you cannot conclude that the human body is inherently evil. There was no evil in Christ's flesh. One could argue that the term human has changed meaning (equivocation). Your body looks human, but the body itself is only part of your humanness. The fact that the meanings are related, one containing the other, suggests that it is not equivocation but a division into the parts. This containment can be helpful in distinguishing equivocations from divisions (and compositions).

Begging the question differs from the last four types in that the relation of a premise and the conclusion is defective, not just the relation between premises. This type of fallacy can be committed explicitly, implicitly, or by using trick questions. An example of each follows.

> **Explicit**—You are too young to go to the store by yourself because you might get killed. You might get killed because you might not be seen by drivers. You might not be seen by drivers because you are not very tall. You are not tall because you are too young.
>
> **Implicit**—Murder is wrong. Therefore, abortion is wrong.
>
> **Trick question**—Have you quit beating your wife?

Notice in the explicit example that the conclusion is stated first. Reasons are given successively (as the child keeps asking "Why?") until one of the reasons given is the conclusion. This shows a clearly circular argument—the conclusion is used as a premise in the proof. Certainly $P \therefore P$ is valid but nothing is proved.

Bear in mind that both the intent and main point of the argument is good. Just a slight change in wording should avoid the fallacy. While speakers (such as this parent) should avoid fallacies, listeners (such as this child) should focus on the main point. Pointing out the fallacy here does not invalidate the intended point.

The implicit example does not explicitly assume what is being proved, but still implies it. The error is more subtle but the point of contention is whether abortion is murder. The argument is actually a transitivity proof in which the debatable point is not stated.

Murder is wrong.

Abortion is murder.

Therefore, abortion is wrong.

This argument is valid, but the second premise will be considered false by many. You must give evidence to convince others that it is murder. Avoiding the issue but assuming it in your argument is begging the question. Assuming what you are trying to prove and pretending that you did not is deception.

The trick question is technically neither a statement nor an argument, but it generates misleading arguments. If the person says, "Yes, I have quit beating my wife," he has admitted that he used to beat her. If he says instead, "No, I have not quit beating my wife," he admits that he is presently beating her. The question poses two alternatives (yes or no), but it results in confession of evil either way. The question "Have you ever beat your wife?" has been answered *yes* for him. This begs the question of his wife beating; he has been assumed guilty without proof. Another famous example of this fallacy is the question "Can God make a rock so big that He can't lift it?"

Formal Fallacies—Formal fallacies have already been discussed. Every time you show a deductive argument false by using a truth table, the deductive argument is a formal fallacy (see Question 5, Chapter 7). The idea here is that there is a defect in the *form* of the argument. This will always become visible in the symbolized form. Remember that the symbols have two major functions—first, to verify (prove) proper deductive argument forms and second, to identify (formal) deductive fallacies. Two major types of formal fallacies will be discussed here: reversed conditionals and improper negations.

First, examine errors of **reversed conditionals.** Recall the two valid arguments based on conditionals: *modus ponens* and *modus tollens.*

Modus Ponens	*Modus Tollens*
$A \rightarrow B$	$A \rightarrow B$
A	$\sim B$
B	$\sim A$

If the second premise is switched with the conclusion, the result is not valid.

$$A \to B \qquad\qquad A \to B$$
$$\underline{B} \qquad\qquad\qquad \underline{\sim A}$$
$$A \qquad\qquad\qquad \sim B$$

These fallacies are called **affirming the consequent** and **denying the antecedent** respectively. The truth table shows that affirming the consequent is invalid:

[(A	→	B)	∧	B]	→	A
T	T	T	T	T	T	T
T	F	F	F	F	T	T
F	T	T	T	T	F	F
F	T	F	F	F	T	F

Notice that the F occurs when A is false and B is true. Here is a real example:

All dogs are mammals.

Fido is a mammal.

Therefore, Fido is a dog.

Now if Fido really is a mammal (B is true), but not a dog (A is false), then the argument fails. If I name my pet cat or my pet kangaroo Fido, I have a counterexample. This means that even when Fido *is* a dog, the argument form does not prove it. The name Fido clouds the issue. You tend to associate Fido with dogs, and so it is easy to overlook the error in reasoning. The name, though, is irrelevant to the symbolism, and the error was identified by the truth table. The fallacy is a formal one. Chapter 4 (Question 8) presented converses, inverses, and contrapositives. You know that the original and the contrapositive are equivalent (contrapositive rule) but are not equivalent to either the converse or the inverse. Do you realize that *modus tollens* arguments use *modus ponens* on the contrapositive? Starting from the premises $A \to B$ and $\sim B$, you can replace the implication with its contrapositive, which is equivalent. Then, *modus ponens* applies to obtain $\sim A$ as shown.

$$\sim B \to \sim A$$
$$\sim B$$
$$\sim A$$

By replacing $A \to B$ with its inverse or converse, you could apply modus ponens to obtain:

$$\sim A \to \sim B \qquad\qquad B \to A$$
$$\sim A \qquad\qquad\qquad B$$
$$\sim B \qquad\qquad\qquad A$$

You should see that denying the antecedent uses *modus ponens* on the inverse, and affirming the consequent uses *modus ponens* on the converse. Both are fallacies because neither the inverse nor the converse are equivalent to the original implication.

Study this example of denying the antecedent:

All dogs are mammals.

Fido is not a dog.

Therefore, Fido is not a mammal.

Notice that this example has the same problem as the previous fallacy. Fido as a mouse or a koala provides a counterexample. You can do the truth table for this one (Question 1).

A second common mistake involves **improper negations.** This is an important class of fallacies. Negations are used in proofs of conditions using contrapositives and in proofs by contradiction (review Chapter 9). In both cases, if the negation is done improperly, a wrong conclusion may result. In fact, errors are sometimes made in negations for *modus tollens* or disjunctive syllogism arguments. Consider the proofs by contradiction: one from a Christian and another from a humanist.

Suppose that all men are good.

In that case, there should be no wars, but there are wars.

Therefore, all men are evil.

Suppose that all men are evil.

In that case, no one would show concern for social injustice, but there are such concerns among many nations.

Therefore, all men are good.

While you may agree with the Christian's conclusion, his argument is just as fallacious as the other. The argument forms are the same.

$M \rightarrow \sim E$	assume for argument	$M \rightarrow \sim G$
$\sim W \ \wedge \ W$	contradiction	$\sim C \ \wedge \ C$
$M \rightarrow E$	law of contradiction	$M \rightarrow G$

Can you see the error? Evil and good are negations, but the negation of "all men are evil" (if man, then evil) is not "all men are good" (if man, then not evil), but rather "some men are good" (man who is not evil . . . $M \wedge \sim E$). In order to prove the case that all men are evil using proof by contradiction, you would assume that some men are good and show that this leads to a contradiction. This is not so easy. If some men are good, some men could still be evil and thus account for the wars. It is far easier to refute "all men are good" (find some that are not) than it is to refute "some men are good" (demonstrate that every man is not good). The arguments are valid if the conclusions are changed to "some men are evil" and "some men are good" respectively. You may be wondering what else is wrong with the second argument, since "some men are good" can't be correct. Do you agree with the premise that evil men do not show any concern for society? If not, then "some men are good" is a valid conclusion, but not a sound one.

In the next chapter, you will learn some other formal fallacies.

Applications

You have seen how formal and informal fallacies arise in daily life. The examples below will show you how they could affect your academic success.

History—Suppose you have to write a short essay on George Washington's presidency. In Chapter 2 you learned that key terms should be defined; however, many other aspects of logic will also influence your grade. Compare these sample paragraphs.

1. George Washington became president of the United States in 1789 at the age of fifty-seven. He was the first president and remained president for two terms. He was unanimously voted president by the electoral college both times. He did not join either of the political parties—Federalists or Republicans (Anti-Federalists). There were some disagreements in both

the cabinet and the Senate about some of his decisions. One such decision was to stay out of the war between France and England in 1793. He toured both the North and the South to learn the problems of his country. His death in 1799 came a few years after his second term had ended. All America mourned and even leaders in Europe paid tribute to his memory.

2. George Washington's presidency displayed his consistent neutrality. Taking office in 1789 at age fifty-seven as the first president, he chose two cabinet members from each of the two political parties. He also toured both the North and the South. As a southerner himself, he maintained neutrality by touring the North first. These measures were successful. He unanimously won the vote of the electoral college for both of his terms in office. He also remained neutral internationally. There were treaties with both England and France, but when those two countries went to war, he refused to aid either. Of the foreign powers he wanted to be ''under the influence of none.'' At the end of his life both countries honored him. George Washington was consistently neutral both at home and abroad.

3. George Washington's presidency shows the tactfulness of a great leader. He became the country's first president at age fifty-seven in 1789. The vote of the electoral college was unanimous. He did not take advantage of his popularity; rather, he appointed four cabinet members—two from each political party. When friction came between Jefferson and Hamilton, he wrote to both of them. When Jefferson eventually resigned, he wrote Jefferson a letter praising his abilities. Washington showed tactfulness in other civil affairs too. He desired to know the problems facing his country, so he toured it. As a southerner, choosing to tour the North first was tactful, not showing favoritism to the South. Every meeting was conducted with solemnity—he was not friendly with some and stern with others. Finally, his foreign policy was tactful. He did not play favorites between France and England. He did not go to the aid of either in the war of 1793. He desired to be ''under the influence of none,'' yet both countries hon-

ored his memory at his death in 1799. George Washington's great leadership was displayed in his tactfulness as president.

4. George Washington, the first president, successfully established the United States of America as an independent world power. He took office in 1789, at age fifty-seven. His success as commanding general in the Revolutionary War gave the people confidence in him as a leader that the world would have to recognize. This explains his first unanimous election (by the electoral college), but the unanimous vote for a second term shows that the people were pleased with his continued leadership. He did not join either of the political parties, and he toured both the North and the South. These attempts to be impartial, together with his solemn public demeanor, gave the nation unity and a sense of dignity in the world. He tried to keep the country from being a puppet to European power. In fact, he ignored a treaty with France when France and England waged war in 1793. He wrote that he desired America to be "under the influence of none." His success both at home and abroad became evident at his death. Not only did his country mourn, but England, France, and others gave tribute.

Which of the four essays on Washington's presidency is best? How does the teacher decide? Give a grade to the essays before you read on. Later you can see how close you are to the way your teacher typically grades. It will help you to know how most teachers grade so that you can write good essays for college or business.

What causes an essay to fail? An essay will automatically fail for any of three reasons. First, **plagiarism** (copying from friends or books without giving credit) spells instant failure. Such dishonesty must be penalized. Second, an essay that does not fulfill the assignment displays **disobedience**. An essay explaining George Washington's battles at New York, Trenton, and Princeton, no matter how good, will fail. The assignment says to write on his presidency. His work in the Revolutionary War preceded his presidency. His work as general may need to be mentioned in some discussions of his work as president but cannot be the main topic of the paper. You must follow directions or fail for disobedience. Finally, some essays fail because they are late, half-done, illegible, have spelling errors, grammatical errors, or mixed-up facts. These kinds of errors display **sloppiness**. This does not always cause failure, but when enough of them are present, the student is telling the teacher that the essay was not important to him. A careless and irresponsible attitude will not be rewarded. No teacher likes to fail students, but lying (plagiarism), disobedience (not following directions), and laziness (sloppiness) are all condemned by Scripture. A Christian teacher must tell the student what God would tell him. Be honest (Col. 3:9), be obedient (Heb. 13:17), and be diligent (Prov. 13:4). Apparently, none of the four essays above will fail.

What causes an essay to be below average (D work)? Usually papers receive Ds because the writer violates basic principles of written communication. Every writer is responsible to:

1. Write essays legibly and punctually.
2. Organize thoughts and paragraphs meaningfully.
3. Report statements accurately.
4. Write sentences grammatically.
5. Spell words correctly.

Violations of these principles confuse the reader. If an essay is not legible, it cannot earn a passing grade from the reader. Likewise, punctuality is crucial for most writers, whether writing for daily newspapers, weekly magazines, quarterly business reports, or annual almanacs. Late news is no longer news. Meaningless rambling to take up space also hinders communication. Remember that false statements make an argument unsound or uncogent automatically and undermine your credibility in the reader's mind. Poor spelling, poor grammar, and lateness reflect irresponsibility. An outline will help to organize your thoughts. Check the accuracy of your facts, spelling, and grammar.

Some teachers try not to grade on spelling or grammar. However, students must realize that frequent errors will interfere with the communication of the content and can still indirectly affect the grade. Other teachers take off a letter grade for spelling, grammatical errors, and lateness. This will mean that an average paper will drop to a D, and even an above average paper can drop to a D if there are many errors or if the paper is very late or both. You can see that all four essays are organized, report factual material accurately, and display good grammar and spelling. Assuming that all four essays were legible and submitted on time, they will pass. To grade these essays, you must look beyond basic principles of communication to logic.

The first thing a reader looks for is a main point. A paper on Washington's presidency should draw some conclusion about his presidency. Read Essay #1 again. It contains a lot of facts, but nothing links the facts together. Every known fact about President Washington could be stated, but the reader still says, "So what?" Do you like it when someone talks on and on and you do not know what he is trying to say? You want to yell, "Get to the point!" The teacher says the same thing to Essay #1. It is not a D or an F essay—the teacher is glad that the student obeyed and did the homework, used reference books, and was accurate and neat. However, it's not a good essay either. The teacher is disappointed that the student did not think about the material and draw a conclusion. The facts held no interest, meaning, or lessons that would go through life with the student. The information he wrote about he will forget tomorrow. Lacking any creative thought, the first essay is just average and gets a C. Notice that its quality is not judged on its length but on its content.

All the other essays did draw conclusions. The students thought about their subjects and really learned. They all got As, right? No! Now you really need logic. Remember that drawing conclusions is reasoning. The teacher must ask whether the essay is well reasoned. Are the arguments supporting the main point valid? Sound? Strong? Cogent?

Essay #2 displays a thoughtful conclusion. This would tend to improve the grade; however, the conclusion is false. The student failed to mention that Washington consistently sided with Hamilton (a Federalist) against Jefferson (a Republican). Washington did that so frequently that Jefferson resigned from the cabinet. This action is anything but consistent neutrality. Either the student made a hasty generalization from the articles he read without knowing it, or he suppressed evidence to make his point sound stronger. Either way his main point hinges on a fallacy. This crucial error means that nothing in his paper is properly linked to anything else. It is still average and gets a C (perhaps C+ for effort or even B if the teacher is being generous on first attempts on essays). A simple change in the first statement to "George Washington sought to be impartial in his presidency" could have made an excellent essay. The fact that Washington did not always succeed would not negate the conclusion that it was his goal. Don't dogmatically overstate your case.

Essay #3 also has a fallacy, but the fallacy supports a minor point. Since the main point is correct, this essay fares better. However, the decision to remain neutral in the 1793 war was not necessarily tactful. It showed favoritism to the Federalist view again and prompted Jefferson's resignation. The statement begs the question. Washington thus broke a treaty with France. Is it tactful to break a treaty? The fact that France did later honor him could be used to argue his tact and wisdom in thus dealing with France, but if his foreign policy was tactful, it certainly requires further support. On the other hand, this questionable point is not the main point. The eleventh, twelfth, and thirteenth sentences could all be omitted, and the other points would not be hurt. The main point would still be well supported. The error will reduce the grade, but the essay is clearly above average. The third essay should get a B (or an A- in a class just learning to write essays).

Essay #4 has no fallacies. The main point is clearly made and supported. There are no fallacies clouding any subpoint. It is unquestionably an A essay.

Notice that the students did not all have to write on the same aspect of his presidency. Other main points that could have been used include "George Washington was a president of principles," "George Washington, as America's first president, gave credibility to the office," or "George Washington set many important precedents as America's first president." All the essays include many of the same facts, but observe that the better essays weave the factual information into the main points and arguments.

How can you improve your essays? Do you see how guidelines will help? First, draw a conclusion and keep that goal in mind as you write. This provides your only chance to do better than a C. Writing with this goal in mind will also help your essay make sense and be organized. Second, plan on rewriting it at least once. Read the first draft again and correct major errors.

1. Is the main point clearly stated? Fix the topic sentence or introduction as needed.

2. What are the reasons for your conclusion? Is each reason organized clearly as a unit (paragraph)? Move sentences or paragraph divisions as needed.
3. Are any of the arguments invalid or weak? Omit or modify such arguments. Modifications may require more reading on the topic.

The above three considerations can make the difference between letter grades. The teacher may not know the name of the fallacy you committed, but your grade will be reduced for poor reasoning. Now read your second draft. Rewrite a second time correcting simpler problems in grammar and spelling if needed. With practice this may not require a second rewrite, but be sure those mistakes get corrected. Finally, be sure you turn it in on time.

Bible—Some errors regarding man's sinfulness have already been noted. Can you find the error in this excerpt from an evangelistic sermon?

> The Bible says in Romans 10:13 'Whosoever shall call upon the name of the Lord shall be saved.' God wrote the Bible and has invited you to be saved. All you have to do is to call on Jesus, according to this verse. So if you don't trust Jesus, you will be damned.

The premises and conclusions here are all true. The problem is that Romans 10:13 does *not* say that Jesus is the only way. It says, "If you call on Jesus, then you are saved." It does *not* say, "If you do not call on Jesus, then you will be damned (not saved)."

Do you see that the second conditional is the inverse of the original? Arguing from the inverse is the fallacy of denying the antecedent. Trusting Jesus is certainly the only way to be saved, but do not imply that this fact is derived from Romans 10:13. Chapter 4 suggested Acts 4:12. Consider also I John 5:12, which asserts both conditionals. Be careful to give people good scriptural support for their beliefs, not invalid support!

Memory Verse—Colossians 2:3, 8-9

> "In whom are hid all the treasures of wisdom and knowledge. Beware lest any man spoil you through philosophy and vain deceit, after the tradition of men, after the rudiments of the world, and not after Christ. For in him dwelleth all the fulness of the Godhead bodily."

The "whom" in verse 3 refers to Jesus Christ. He has all wisdom and knowledge. He is the *truth* (John 14:6). Ultimately only He can protect you from committing or propagating fallacies. Trust Him for wisdom to recognize fallacies so that you are not misled. Be careful to "prove all things, and hold fast that which is good."

Conclusion

There are many problems in deductive argumentation. False premises, such as a false dichotomy, are not fallacies but make the deductive argument unsound. Formal fallacies can be identified using truth tables or Venn diagrams. Informal fallacies appear correct in truth tables but have more subtle errors that are found only by studying the context. Informal fallacies include accident, equivocation, composition, division, and begging the question. Two kinds of formal fallacies were introduced: fallacies of conditionals and negations. The chart summarizes the main fallacies studied in this chapter.

False Premises	Fallacies	
	Informal	**Formal**
False dichotomy	Accident	Reversed conditionals
	Equivocation	Improper negations
	Composition	
	Division	
	Begging the question	

Two examples of reversed conditionals were discussed: denying the antecedent and affirming the consequent. Three types of begging the question were presented: explicit, implicit, and the trick question.

You have seen how these errors hurt your essay writing and Bible teaching. Even if you forget the names of the fallacies, you must recognize when they are committed and avoid them. Keeping the main point in mind, arguing carefully, and rewriting after proofreading will help reduce errors and improve your work.

Remember that all wisdom and knowledge are in Christ. Be careful not to be fooled by false reasoning.

Finally, review the points regarding good essays. First, draw a conclusion and stick to it as you write. An outline can help you organize your thoughts. Second, reread your rough draft and correct logical errors including the clarity of your main point, the organization of your main lines of support, and the strength or validity of each line of support. Third, review your rewrite, making sure to check spelling, grammar, and legibility. Type it if possible and get it in on time.

You can see that a good grade requires good logic.

A - Main point is true; good arguments support it.

B - Main point is true; some supporting arguments are good, but others are weak.

C - Main point is lacking or without supporting evidence. Factual information is reported meeting the minimum requirements of the assignment.

D - No main point. Factual information does not fulfill the assignment.

F - Either (1) the directions are not followed or (2) plagiarism is evident.

Teachers may reduce grades for sloppy and irresponsible work of the following types: illegibility, lateness, disorganized rambling, inaccurate factual information, and poor spelling or grammar. These violations of basic principles of writing hinder understanding, undermine credibility, and demonstrate a lack of responsibility. The number or degree of such mistakes will determine how far a B essay drops, ranging from no drop at all (inconsequential), to one letter grade, or all the way to an F.

Terms

accident
affirming the consequent
begging the question
composition
denying the antecedent
disobedience
division

equivocation
explicit begging the question (or *petitio principii*)
false dichotomy
formal fallacy
implicit begging the question (or *circulus in probando*)
improper negation
informal fallacy
plagiarism
reversed conditional
sloppiness
trick question (or *plurium interrogationum*)

Questions

1. Make a truth table to show that denying the antecedent is a fallacy.
2. Match the deductive arguments.

1. Valid and sound	A. fallacy
2. Valid and unsound	B. good argument
3. Invalid and sound	C. impossible
4. Invalid and unsound	D. false premise

3. Find a false dichotomy in an advertisement.
   (Example: Buy Sparkle toothpaste or get cavities!)
4. Informal fallacies (and false premises): Match the error to each deductive argument.

1. IBM is very professional because each employee is well qualified.	A. Accident
	B. Begging the Question
2. Ford cars are great since all the mechanics are great.	C. Composition
	D. Division
3. Blow up the Commies or they will attack, and then it will be too late.	E. Equivocation
	F. False Dichotomy
4. Newsmen have the right to publish government secrets because freedom of speech is guaranteed by law.	

5. The Bible is literally true, and it refers to sunrise and sunset. So the sun must orbit the earth and modern science must be wrong.

5. Formal Fallacies: Identify each formal fallacy.

   a. Some men are liars, since it is false that some men are not liars.

   b. Liars are killers. Joe is not a liar, so Joe is not a killer.

   c. All killers are liars by nature and Jeff is a liar. Therefore, Jeff is a killer also.

6. Is the fallacy below formal or informal? Explain your answer.

   $A \rightarrow B$ and $C \rightarrow B$. Therefore, $A \rightarrow C$.

7. Amphiboly is a special type of equivocation. Usually it is not intentional. Read the argument and explain the problem.
   You were warned about frequent errors in this chapter. Therefore, the chapter must be carelessly written.

8. What error is made by the Sadducees in Matthew 22:28?

9. Write an essay on Lincoln's presidency. Include both the rough draft and the rewrite.

10. Write an essay on Gottlob Frege. What was his contribution to logic? Defend your position and avoid fallacies.

CHAPTER 12
Tools for Reasoning

How many tools for reasoning can you name that you have studied so far? You should recognize that truth tables and diagrams provided graphic representations of principles that everything else was built upon. Symbolic logic is the tool you have used the most and which took the most effort to learn. You learned to represent arguments with symbols to help you understand claims and lines of reasoning. You have also used symbolic logic to derive new rules of logic from previously established rules. Another tool that you have learned is classification. You can classify definitions, statements, categoricals, arguments, and fallacies. Classifications of arguments and fallacies are useful aids in evaluating arguments.

Concepts

This chapter will expand your knowledge of logic by developing skills with quantification and categoricals.

Quantification—The first topic involves **quantifiers.** Remember that the terms *universal* and *particular* refer to the quantity of a categorical. Thus, the words *all, some,* and *no* are called quantifiers. In mathematics "for all" is symbolized by $\forall$, and "some" (meaning "there exists") is symbolized by $\exists$. While you will not need these two symbols in this book, you should recognize them. For now, consider the rules and fallacies governing quantification. This class of fallacies will be called **quantifier mistakes.** These fallacies occur when *all, some, no,* and related terms are misused. In Chapter 11, you saw a quantifier mistake due to an improper negation, but here the mistakes in quantifiers occur for other reasons. The two types of quantifier mistakes are the universal generalization fallacy and the existential instantiation fallacy. To recognize these fallacies, some background is necessary. Consider the argument below.

All men are sinners.

Therefore, if Jack is a man, then Jack is a sinner.

This argument turns the universal statement into a conditional statement. The name Jack may refer to a specific person or a representative person (as when you use x, John Smith, etc.). This is called **universal instantiation (UI)** because it replaces the universal principle with an instance of the principle. Thus far, you have been doing this mentally without acknowledging the rule.

The reverse process begins with a particular instance and makes a generalization from it. Since the conclusion is universal, it is called **universal generalization (UG).**

If John is a man, then John is a sinner.

Therefore, all men are sinners.

This argument commits a fallacy. It is silly to conclude that all men are sinners, just because one man is. Could you say, "Wong is Chinese; therefore, all men are Chinese?" This mistake is the **universal generalization fallacy (UGF).** Is universal generalization always a fallacy? No; however, one must be very careful in order to avoid the fallacy. To succeed, "John" must not be a specific individual, but a representative of any person in the class. In this case, since John can represent any man and since his sinfulness is established, the argument correctly concludes that all have sinned. In prose, you attempt to establish representativeness in various ways such as "Suppose someone is a doctor. . ." or "Once upon a time there was a doctor." Such a phrase often portrays a generic doctor. Be careful; there is a fine line between the valid universal generalization and the universal generalization fallacy. The difference lies in whether the name is specific or representative. By contrast, a universal instantiation is not tricky; it is always valid.

Consider the following argument:

Pete is a sinner.

Therefore, some people are sinners (i.e., there is a sinner).

Of course, this argument is valid. If you identify an example of a group, then there must be things in that group. If a unicorn were ever spotted (and verified), the one sighting would show that "Some animals are unicorns" and that unicorns exist (there is a unicorn). This is **existential generalization (EG);** it makes a generalization about the existence of something.

The reverse situation **existential instantiation (EI)** is again tricky. Typically, it results in a fallacy:

> Some people are sinners (or there is a sinner).
>
> Thus, Bruce is a sinner.

This is the **existential instantiation fallacy (EIF).** The fact that sinners exist does not make Bruce one of them. You would see the mistake more clearly by replacing ''Bruce'' with ''Jesus''! Is existential instantiation ever valid? Yes; you can say, ''I once knew a sinner; let's call him Bruce.'' This statement has the same form as the argument above. The difference is that the name Bruce is used to represent the thing guaranteed to exist by the premise. The fallacy occurred because ''Bruce'' had a previous particular meaning. If ''Bruce'' is a real person or has any meaning in the context, the fallacy has been committed. If ''Bruce'' is instead understood as representative—newly chosen for purpose of discussion only— then the conclusion is valid. Like before, there is a fine line between a valid existential instantiation and the existential instantiation fallacy. Again, by contrast, an existential generalization is never a fallacy.

You have seen four types of quantified arguments. You can classify each argument by the quantifier in the categorical statement. If the quantifier is *all,* it is universal; if it is *some,* it is existential. You can also classify these quantified arguments by the generalization or instantiation of their conclusions. In a generalization the conclusion is general, a categorical statement (*all* or *some*); whereas, in an instantiation the conclusion is specific, involving an example or instance, Q. The following table summarizes these facts. The table will also remind you about the fallacies that can result from two of the types.

	Conclusion Type	
Categorical involved	**Generalization**	**Instantiation**
Universal	If Q is A, then Q is B; therefore, *all* A are B.	All A are B; therefore, if Q is A, then Q is B.
	Validity: sometimes	Validity: always
	Fallacy: occurs when Q is not a generic representative of the class A.	Fallacy: never
Existential	Q is a B; therefore, some A are B.	Some A are B; therefore, Q is a B.
	Validity: always	Validity: sometimes
	Fallacy: never	Fallacy: occurs when Q refers to reality or already has meaning in the context

The two fallacies may seem subtle, but they can be detected by using symbolic forms beyond the scope of this book. For this reason, they are formal fallacies in spite of the subtlety.

You already know about the four types of categorical statements, and you also know that a syllogism is an argument with two premises and a conclusion. When the premises of the argument and the conclusion are categorical statements, it is called a **categorical syllogism.** Do you remember the categoricals: "All A are B" (universal), "No A are B" (universal negative), "Some A are B" (particular), and "Some A are not B" (particular negative)? The rules for evaluating the validity of categorical syllogisms are very useful. Each rule, when broken, results in a fallacy. There are seven fallacies for categorical syllogisms. If a syllogism does not commit any of the seven fallacies, then it does not break any of the rules, and it is valid. One tool that will help you visualize the fallacies in the syllogisms is Venn diagramming. Consider the use of Venn diagrams in the following statements. The rectangle is the universe. The circles represent the sets containing A and B as labeled.

All *A* are *B*.

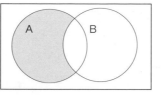

Cross out (with shading) the section of *A* that is not in *B*. Now the only *A*'s left are inside the *B* circle.

No *A* are *B*.

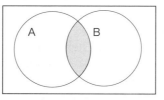

This time *A* and *B* should not overlap, so cross out the section of *A*'s that are also *B*'s.

Some *A* are *B*.

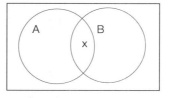

Remember that "some" means "at least one." Use an *x* to show the existence of one item that is both an *A* and a *B*.

Some *A* are not *B*.

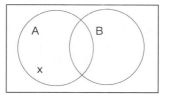

This time the one *A* is not in set *B*.

Consider the argument below:

No *A* are *B*.

All *C* are *B*.

Some *C* are not *A*.

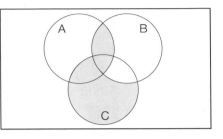

By diagramming the premises only, you can see that the premises do not provide any instances. There is no *x* in the diagram. The conclusion must be faulty because the diagram does not show an *x* in the *A* and *C* overlap region. The conclusion is not guaranteed by the premises; when particular claims are made from universal premises, the argument commits the **existential fallacy.**

Compare the following arguments:

No fish are dogs.

All collies are dogs.

Some collies are not fish.

No bees are white.

All unicorns are white.

Some unicorns are not bees.

Both of these commit the fallacy, but the first does not seem objectionable because you know that collies are real. However, the second concludes that there is a unicorn that is not a bee, and this is false even though you agree with the premises. Since the entire overlap between *A* and *C* is crossed out, the correct conclusion to the argument is that ''No *A* are *C*.'' You may notice other relations in the diagram, but they are the premises. The conclusion must relate *A* and *C,* the terms *not* related in either premise. The rule, then, is that a particular conclusion requires a particular premise. Fallacies are usually not identified as existential if one of the next six fallacies are also present. For this reason, this rule is best to list last.

The fallacy of **exclusive premises** occurs when both premises are negative. No correct conclusion can be drawn in such a case. Rule 1 requires at least one premise to be affirmative. For example, by diagramming the two premises shown, you see that no valid conclusion relating dogs and goats is possible.

No dogs are pigs.

Some pigs are not goats.

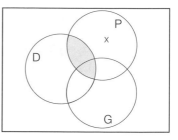

The next two fallacies are related. They describe the two ways of breaking Rule 2: the conclusion is negative if and only if one premise is negative.

All dogs are mammals.

Some dogs are collies.

Some mammals are not collies.

Fallacy: negative conclusion
Valid conclusion: Some
  mammals are collies.

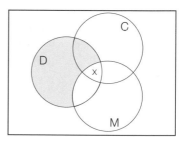

The **negative conclusion** fallacy occurs if the conclusion is negative and both premises are affirmative. The **affirmative conclusion** fallacy occurs when the conclusion is affirmative and either premise is negative. Notice in the following examples that the conclusion is invalid.

Some dogs are not collies.

Some dogs are brown.

Some collies are brown.

Fallacy: affirmative conclusion
Valid conclusion: not
possible

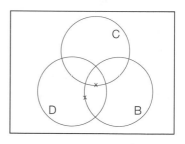

The *x* appears on the line in the diagram because the brown dog may or may not be a collie. It cannot be placed inside or outside the *C* circle with certainty. Since it is not necessarily inside the *C* circle, the argument does not prove that there is a brown collie. If you accept the conclusion, it is not based on the reasoning given.

The last three fallacies for categorical syllogisms will require one last tool besides diagramming. You must recognize which sets are completely involved in a statement; this is called **distribution.** Do not confuse distribution of sets in categoricals with distribution of connectives from Chapter 5.

Some A are B.	Neither A nor B is distributed. It identifies only one element in either set.
Some A are not B.	Only set B is distributed. It refers to only one element of set A, which is distinguished from every element of B. Set B is completely involved.
All A are B.	Only set A is distributed. Every element of A is in B, but B may contain others. Set B is not completely involved.
No A are B.	Both A and B are distributed.

With this in mind, you can understand the last fallacies.

The fallacy of the **undistributed middle** occurs when the middle term (the one in both premises) is not distributed in either premise.

All A are B.
Some B are not C.

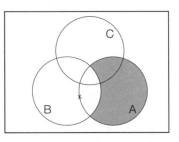

No conclusion is possible, since B is not distributed in either premise (although both A and C are). The elements of B that are in A may or may not be the same ones that are not C:

All dogs are mammals.	All dogs are mammals.
Some mammals are not camels.	Some mammals are not collies.

You can see that an undistributed middle term breaks Rule 3: The middle term must be distributed in at least one premise.

The final principle, Rule 4, states that any term distributed in the conclusion must be distributed in a premise. The subject of the conclusion is called the minor term; the predicate noun of the conclusion is called the major term. Thus, two fallacies arise, depending on which term breaks the rule.

> All dogs are mammals.
> Some poodles are dogs.
> Therefore, all poodles are mammals.

The problem in this example is **illicit minor**, because the minor term, "poodle," is distributed in the conclusion but not in the premise that contains it. Notice that no other rule is violated in the argument. Now, consider one final example.

> All dogs are mammals.
> Some poodles are dogs.
> Therefore, some mammals are not poodles.

In this argument the major term, "poodles," is distributed in the conclusion but not in the premise. This is an **illicit major.** This time the negative conclusion fallacy has also been committed. It is important to recognize that "mammals" was not distributed in the first premise. However, that does not in itself create a fallacy. Since "mammals" was not distributed in the conclusion, it did not need to be distributed in either premise.

Applications

You have already seen examples of quantification and categorical syllogisms. Mathematics provides an example of how crucial they are.

Mathematics—Marcia, a beginning geometry student, knows the following three geometry principles:

1. If there are two points, there is a point between them.
2. If there are two points, there is a midpoint between them.
3. If there is a point on a line, there is a perpendicular to the line at the point.

Suppose Marcia wants to prove that every segment has a perpendicular bisector. Her proof follows:

1. Two points A and B and the joining segment $\overline{AB}$ are given.	1. assumption for conditional proof
2. Let C be a point between A and B on $\overleftrightarrow{AB}$.	2. Principle 1 (*modus ponens,* then existential instantiation for point C)
3. Let l be a line perpendicular to $\overleftrightarrow{AB}$ at C.	3. Principle 3 (*modus ponens,* then existential instantiation for line l)
4. Let C be the midpoint of $\overline{AB}$.	4. Principle 2 (*modus ponens,* then existential instantiation for point C)
5. There is a perpendicular bisector of $\overline{AB}$.	5. existential generalization, (namely, line l)
6. If $\overline{AB}$ is a segment, then $\overleftrightarrow{AB}$ has a perpendicular bisector.	6. conditional proof
7. All segments have perpendicular bisectors.	7. universal generalization

First, to apply the geometry principles, Marcia used instantiation rules. *Modus ponens* from Step 1 actually shows that "There is a point between A and B." Existential instantiation is needed to name this point C. Likewise, in Step 3, the name for line l also requires existential instantiation. The fallacy occurs at line 4. The midpoint has been named C, but C has meaning already. C is a point between A and B, but not necessarily the midpoint. When the existential instantiation fallacy is pointed out, Marcia may try to correct the proof by erasing Step 2. This creates another problem: line 3 raises a perpendicular at C, but C has no meaning without Step 2. The solution is to put Step 4 in place of Step 2. Principle 1 is not needed in this proof, and the order of application of the other two principles is very important.

Bible—Remember that God gave man dominion over the earth. God expects man to use the tools available to him as a good steward. Your use of biblical principles is an important tool in your stewardship. You also use biblical principles when you test commonly held views against Scripture. Some people argue that music is amoral or neutral. Test their syllogism against Scripture.

Whatever can be used for good or for evil is in itself neutral.

Music can be used for good or evil.

Therefore, music is neutral.

You should see that this argument is a universal instantiation, which is always valid. The syllogism is not sound though, since the first premise is false. Can you see why it is false?

Can rocks, trees, and school subjects be used for good and evil? Of course, but are they neutral? No! God declared rocks very good at the end of the week of creation (see Gen. 1:31), even though rocks could be used for building both temples for God and temples for idols. Likewise, even though Adam and Eve misused the fruit of the tree of the knowledge of good and evil, God saw that it was good when He made it. Everything God creates reflects its Creator, and these things are good. Be sure you use God's good gifts for good and not for evil.

Is logic good, evil, or neutral?

Memory Verse—John 16:13

"Howbeit when he, the Spirit of truth, is come, he will guide you into all truth: for he shall not speak of himself; but whatsoever he shall hear, that shall he speak: and he will shew you things to come."

This verse shows that the Holy Spirit has a key role in guiding you to truth. He will never guide you to misuse biblical principles or to substitute human views for truth.

Conclusion

Venn diagrams use circles to represent the sets in categorical statements. Shading is used to cross out parts of sets, while an *x* is used to represent a particular element of a set.

Another tool for analyzing categorical syllogisms is distribution. The *A* and *B* terms are differently distributed by each type of categorical as shown in the following chart.

		A	
		distributed	not distributed
B	distributed	No *A* are *B*.	Some *A* are not *B*.
	not distributed	All *A* are *B*.	Some *A* are *B*.

The tools mentioned above result in five rules for categorical syllogisms. Rule 5 is used only if none of the first four apply.

Rule	Rules for Categorical Syllogisms	Corresponding Fallacies
1.	At least one premise must be affirmative.	Exclusive premises
2.	The conclusion is negative if and only if one premise is negative.	Affirmative conclusion Negative conclusion
3.	The middle term must be distributed in at least one premise.	Undistributed middle
4.	Any term distributed in the conclusion must be distributed in a premise.	Illicit major Illicit minor
5.	A particular conclusion requires a particular premise.	Existential fallacy

The other tool discussed in the chapter was quantification. The four quantifier rules are as follows:

Rule	Explanation
1. Universal Instantiation (UI)	applies universal principle
2. Existential Generalization (EG)	claims existence from example
3. Universal Generalization (UG)	claims principle from representative example
4. Existential Instantiation (EI)	applies existence to label a representative

The first two quantifier rules are always valid; the last two result in fallacies if restrictions are ignored.

| Universal Generalization Fallacy (UGF) | occurs if the example is not a generic representative |
| Existential Instantiation Fallacy (EIF) | occurs if the label already has meaning in context |

Terms

affirmative conclusion

categorical syllogism

distribution

exclusive premises

existential fallacy

Existential Generalization

Existential Instantiation

Existential Instantiation Fallacy

illicit major

illicit minor

negative conclusion

quantification

undistributed middle

Universal Generalization

Universal Generalization Fallacy

Universal Instantiation

Questions

Answer Questions 1 and 2 using the argument below.

> Some *A* are *C*.
>
> Some *B* are *C*.
> _____
>
> No *A* are *B*.

1. Identify the
   a. middle term
   b. minor term
   c. major term
2. Is it valid? Which fallacies are committed?

Make truth tables to show that each argument commits a fallacy.

   3. Undistributed middle

      All *A* are *B*.

      All *C* are *B*.

      All *A* are *C*.

   4. Illicit minor

      All *A* are *B*.

      All *A* are *C*.

      All *B* are *C*.

Give Venn diagrams and valid conclusions for the arguments below.

   5.   All cows are vegetarians.

        Some athletes are not vegetarians.

        Therefore, . . .

   6.   All dentists are professionals.

        Some dentists are Christians.

        Therefore, . . .

   7.   No kings are tornados.

        All chess pieces are tornados.

        Therefore, . . .

   8. **Quantification.** Classify each of the following six quantifier arguments, using an abbreviation selected from this list; UI, UG, EI, EG, UIF, UGF, EIF, EGF. Single letters represent the following: F, fallacy; U, universal; E, existential; I, instantiation; G, generalization.

     1) Joe Average Minnesotan is created by God and is therefore loved by God. Thus, all Minnesotans are loved by God.

     2) If a person lives in Minnesota, then he likes hockey. Therefore, if Barton Flugelberg lives in Minnesota, then Barton must like hockey.

3) There are lakes in Minnesota with good bass fishing and there are lakes in Minnesota with good trout fishing. One of these lakes with both good bass fishing and good trout fishing is called Fish Lake.

4) At Clear Lake in Minnesota there is excellent muskie fishing. Thus, there are lakes in Minnesota with good muskie fishing.

5) There are lakes in Minnesota with good bass fishing. We will refer to one of these as Bass Lake; the story could have happened at any such lake in Minnesota, but actual identities are being held in confidence.

6) Marlene Petersen is an average Minnesotan. She works part-time and has two children. She tolerates the cold winters well. Therefore, all Minnesotans tolerate cold winters well.

9. Match the following **Formal Fallacies.** None are used more than once.

1) Some men are liars and some liars are killers. Therefore, some men are killers.

2) All victims are children and all children are human. Therefore, some humans are not victims.

3) Some men lie and some men kill. Therefore, some men both lie and kill.

4) Some men are killers and some pastors are not killers. Therefore, some men are not pastors.

5) All lunar nations are ancient and all ancient nations are powerful. Thus, some lunar nations are powerful.

A. affirmative conclusion

B. negative conclusion

C. undistributed middle

D. illicit major

E. illicit minor

F. exclusive premises

G. existential fallacy

H. Universal Generalization Fallacy

I. Existential Instantiation Fallacy

6) There is a man who knows everything. Thus, all men know everything.

7) Some brilliant people are not happy. No sick people are happy. Therefore, some brilliant people are not sick.

10. Write a paragraph about John Venn. Use your knowledge of essays to write an appropriate one.

Review Questions

Chapter 1: Purposes of Definition

1. Match each example to the best classification. Use each answer once.

   1. *College* means a ledge or cliff where people have camped using a coal fire.

   2. *College* means a society of persons with a common pursuit, especially educational; a specialty school, university subdivision, or its buildings.

   3. *College* (for purposes of the State Board of Higher Education) means an educational center that offers associate's and bachelor's degrees, but not graduate degrees.

   4. *College* means a mission endeavor which promotes a specific philosophy through recruitment (evangelization) and classroom training (teaching).

   A. Characterizing

   B. Convincing

   C. Clarifying

   D. Creating

Chapter 2: Methods of Definition

2. Match each sample definition to the technique used.

1. *College* means a place where you go to study away from home for four years after high school.

2. *College*, from the Latin word for "association," came to refer to institutions offering only bachelor's degrees. It is now often used broadly to refer to all institutions of higher learning whether public or private, secular or religious.

3. *College* means an educational center.

4. *College* means Northland Baptist, Southern Oregon State, and Amherst.

5. *College* means an institution for training after high school.

A. Development

B. Example

C. Classification

D. Synonym

Chapter 3: Sentence Types

3. For each sentence from Colossians, determine the most appropriate designation for the type of sentence.

1. That ye might walk worthy of the Lord unto all pleasing. (1:10)

2. And he is before all things, and by him all things consist. (1:17)

3. Why, as though living in the world, are ye subject to ordinances? (2:20)

4. Set your affections on things above, not on things on the earth. (3:2)

5. Amen. (4:18)

A. Statement

B. Exclamation

C. Question

D. Command

E. Request

Chapter 4: Truth Tables

4. Make truth tables for both expressions.

    a. $(A \lor B) \land (A \to B)$ b. $(A \leftrightarrow B) \to \sim(A \land B)$

Chapter 5: Equivalences

5. For each expression below, match the correct negation.

1. $\sim A$	A. Some A are B.
2. $A \lor B$	B. Some A are not B.
3. $A \to B$	C. No A are B.
4. $\sim A \land B$	D. A
5. $A \land B$	E. $\sim A$
6. All A are B.	F. $A \land \sim B$
7. Some A are not B.	G. $A \lor \sim B$
8. No A are B.	H. $\sim A \land \sim B$
	I. $A \to B$
	J. $\sim A \lor \sim B$

Chapter 6: Induction

6. Match the argument to its method.

1. We suspect that the city of Atlanta will permit the zoning of a new Hindu temple, because our survey shows that Atlanta is over 80% Hindu.	A. Authority
	B. Utility
2. According to the world almanac, South Asia is less than 2% Protestant. South Asia apparently has a great need for Protestant missions.	C. Experience
	D. Silence
3. Since no one can go back to the beginning of the earth, no scientist can say for sure that God did not create it.	E. Analogy
	F. Tendency
4. Well, Jeff, that must be the right way to compute areas of sectors because we get the same answers as the book.	
5. I had to cancel our picnic because it rained. I guess Murphy's Law is true.	

Chapter 7: Deduction

7. Match each argument to its method.

1. Since love implies patience and since God is love, we can conclude that God is patient.

2. Since love is good, then either love or sin is good.

3. Since either love or sin is good and since sin is evil, it must be that love is good.

4. A person is justified if he accepts Christ as his Savior. Since all who are justified are glorified, it follows that accepting Christ guarantees glorification.

5. Since Christ justifies the saved and since He glorifies the saved, we see that Christ both justifies and glorifies the saved.

A. Addition Argument

B. Conjunctive Syllogism

C. Disjunctive Syllogism

D. *Modus Ponens*

E. *Modus Tollens*

F. Simplification Argument

G. Transitivity Argument

Chapter 8: Theories

8. Match each theory to the most important criterion that it fails to meet. Use each answer once. (Remember to check for them in order.)

1. Man is inherently good (humanism).

2. The only cause of cancer is smoking.

3. The planets move because angels guide them on their paths at the correct speed.

4. The planets move in circular orbits about the earth, but epicycles (suborbits) account for the backward motions.

5. Fossils are dated by the strata in which they are found. Fossils found in lower strata are considered older unless they are more complex organisms. Such organisms show that there were uplifts and overthrusts among rock layers (uniformitarianism).

6. Living things can progress from less to more complex forms (evolution).

7. Suction was conceived as an application of the principle that "nature does not permit vacuums."

A. Harmony with Scripture

B. Coherence

C. Adequacy

D. Consistency

E. Simplicity

F. Accuracy

G. Fruitfulness

Chapter 9: Hypothetical Deductive Arguments

9. Match each argument to its method.

1. The Jews knew the law. When they disobeyed the law, God punished them. If a person knows the law, then he is more responsible to obey and please God. (paraphrasing of Rom. 2:17-29)

2. The apostle Paul was a Jew and was saved (Acts 9). Simon the sorcerer was a Samaritan and was saved (8:5-14). Gentiles are people who are not Jews or Samaritans. Cornelius was a Gentile and was saved (10:1-11:1). Therefore, people of all nations can be saved.

3. The flood shows that the scoffer's position that "all things happen gradually" is false. (See II Peter 3:3-6)

4. Suppose that baptism is required for salvation. If this were so, then people who were not baptized would have to go to hell. The thief on the cross went to paradise (Luke 23:43); however, he was saved while dying and could not get baptized. Also, Mark 16:16 gives lack of belief as the sole cause of damnation. Therefore, baptism is not required for salvation.

A. Law of Cases

B. Law of Contradiction

C. Law of Deduction

D. Counterexample

Chapter 10: Inductive Fallacies

10. Match the best description to each inductive argument. Answers may be used more than once.

A. Strong and cogent

B. Weak and cogent

C. Strong and uncogent

D. Weak and uncogent: unqualified authority

E. Weak and uncogent: appeal to ignorance

F. Weak and uncogent: hasty generalization

G. Weak and uncogent: strained analogy

H. Weak and uncogent: exceptional experience

I. Weak and uncogent: false cause

J. Weak and uncogent: missing the point

K. Weak and uncogent: appeal to the people

L. Weak and uncogent: appeal to pity

M. Weak and uncogent: straw man

1. Parrots can perch like an owl; therefore, they probably have keen night vision like an owl.

2. Out of 500 birds surveyed in Cincinnati city parks, 250 of them were parrots. Therefore, probably about half of the birds in the Cincinnati vicinity are parrots.

3. Parrots can kill pythons, and just because biologists have not observed it does not mean that it does not happen.

4. No wild parrots have ever been spotted in Minnesota; therefore, parrots are not native to Minnesota.

5. No wild parrots have been seen in Maine, Minnesota, or Montana. So they are probably not native to the U.S.

6. The parrots chirp happily when Joe, the feeder, enters the parrot cage. Therefore, the parrots must like Joe.

7. Both parrots and macaws are long-tailed tropical birds with curved beaks and similar nesting habits. Therefore, they probably also have similar feeding habits.

8. The zoo custodian, who cleans the bird exhibit, says that parrots can be found in Siberia and Norway. These areas indicate an amazing range for a primarily tropical bird.

9. We found three white (albino) parrots in our survey of 1,000 parrots in Brazil. Therefore, probably about 0.3% of the Brazilian parrots are white.

10. You really should buy another parrot: Polly looks so lonely in there.

11. The pastor said, "You must accept Christ to be saved." This is as much as saying that man has more control over his destiny than God. Such extreme Arminianism is not biblical, so the pastor is misleading people.

12. The pastor said, "Accept Christ this morning and leave the church forever a child of God." Therefore, he must be liberal since he encourages people not to come back to church.

Chapter 11: Deductive Fallacies

11. Match the best answer to each of the following deductive arguments.

A. Valid and sound
B. Valid and unsound: false dichotomy
C. Valid and unsound: other reason
D. Invalid and sound
E. Invalid and unsound: accident
F. Invalid and unsound: affirmative conclusion
G. Invalid and unsound: affirming the consequent
H. Invalid and unsound: begging the question

I. Invalid and unsound: composition
J. Invalid and unsound: denying the antecedent
K. Invalid and unsound: division
L. Invalid and unsound: equivocation
M. Invalid and unsound: existential fallacy
N. Invalid and unsound: existential instantiation fallacy
O. Invalid and unsound: illicit minor
P. Invalid and unsound: universal generaliza - tion fallacy

1. The Bible says, "Thou shalt not kill"; therefore, I will refuse all military service.

2. To be green is to be envious. Parrots are green; therefore, parrots are envious.

3. Pastor, when will people start being more friendly at this church?

4. Parrots are dogs, and Fido is a parrot. Therefore, Fido is a dog.

5. Pastor, either you let me teach Sunday school or you force me to change churches.

6. Parrots are birds, and Fido is not a parrot. Thus, Fido is not a bird.

7. Parrots are birds, and Fido is a parrot. Therefore, Fido is a bird.

8. Parrots are green; therefore, each feather on them is completely green.

9. The winner of the Olympic downhill skiing medal was a great athlete and was very fast. Therefore, to be a great athlete you must be very fast.

10. Parrots are birds, and no dogs are birds. Therefore, all dogs are parrots.

Chapter 12: Reasoning Tools

12. Make Venn diagrams for the following.

   a.   Diagram ''Some mothers are students.''

Diagram each argument and supply the valid conclusion.

   b.   All beautiful places are photogenic (places).
         All forests are beautiful (places).

   c.   No rivers are oceans.
         All streams are rivers.

   d.   Some wildernesses are mountainous (places).
         No wildernesses are boring (places).

Categoricals

13. "All parrots are birds" is a statement. Identify the related statements by matching.

    1. Inverse
    2. Contrapositive
    3. Negation
    4. Universal Instantiation
    5. Converse

    A. No parrots are birds.
    B. Some parrots are not birds.
    C. Some parrots are birds.
    D. All birds are parrots.
    E. If it is not a bird, then it is not a parrot.
    F. If it is not a parrot, then it is not a bird.
    G. If Polly is a parrot, then Polly is a bird.

Symbolic Logic

14. Complete the proofs of the statements shown by supplying the step or reason as indicated. The eight possible reasons are listed at right with their abbreviations. Be sure to include premise numbers in reasons.

MP	*Modus Ponens*	CS	Conjunctive Syllogism
MT	*Modus Tollens*	SA	Simplification Argument
DS	Disjunctive Syllogism	AA	Addition Argument
TA	Transitivity Argument	CD	Constructive Dilemma

A. Prove ~A

    1. $C \lor (A \to B)$ premise

    2. ~$C \land$ ~B premise

    3. ~C _____

    4. ~$B \land$ ~C Commutative Law for Conjunction (premise 2)

    5. _____   SA (premise 4)

    6. _____   _____

    7. _____   _____

B. Prove $B \vee N$

1.	$(M \vee N) \rightarrow (F \rightarrow G)$	given
2.	$D \rightarrow {\sim}C$	given
3.	${\sim}C \rightarrow B$	given
4.	M	given
5.	$D \vee F$	given
6.	$D \rightarrow B$	_____
7.	$M \vee N$	_____
8.	$F \rightarrow G$	_____
9.	$(D \rightarrow B) \wedge (F \rightarrow G)$	_____
10.	$B \vee G$	_____

Hypothetical Reasoning

15. The following proofs make use of a few of the rules of replacement as well as the eight basic rules of inference. All rules are listed below for your convenience. Include the step number for each premise with your reasons.

Rules of Inference		**Rules of Replacement**	
MP	*Modus Ponens*	BR	Biconditional Rule
MT	*Modus Tollens*	CR	Contrapositive Rule
DS	Disjunctive Syllogism	DC	Distribution of Conjunction
TA	Transitivity Argument	DD	Distribution of Disjunction
CS	Conjunctive Syllogism	DN	Double Negation
SA	Simplification Argument	NC	Negation of Conjunction
AA	Addition Argument	ND	Negation of Disjunction
CD	Constructive Dilemma	NI	Negation of Implication

Of course, you may also use commutative and associative laws as well as the laws of deduction, cases, and contradiction.

Review Questions

A. Prove $(C \wedge D) \to F$
1. $(D \wedge C) \to E$ given
2. $(D \wedge E) \to F$ given
   3. $D \wedge C$ assumed
   4. E _____
   5. D _____
   6. $D \wedge E$ _____
   7. F _____
8. $(D \wedge C) \to F$ _____
9. $(C \wedge D) \to F$ _____

B. Prove $S \wedge R$
1. $(S \wedge D) \vee (S \wedge H)$ given
2. $S \to R$ given
   3. $\sim(S \wedge R)$ _____
   4. $\sim S \vee \sim R$ _____
   5. $S \wedge (D \vee H)$ _____
   6. S _____
   7. $\sim\sim S$ _____
   8. $\sim R$ _____
   9. R _____
   10. $R \wedge \sim R$ _____
11. $S \wedge R$ _____

16. Which concept did you find most helpful?

   A. Methods and purposes of definition
   B. Sentence and statement types
   C. Induction methods and deduction forms
   D. Criteria for theories and laws of proof
   E. Fallacies of induction and deduction
   F. Truth tables for connectives
   G. Venn diagrams
   H. Proofs
   I. Rules of categorical syllogisms
   J. Rules of quantifiers

Afterword

You have completed your introduction to logic. Definitions of words formed the foundation for your study. No communication is successful unless meaning is clear. Next you studied truth. Words combine to form sentences. Statements are the types of sentences needed in discussion, justification, and persuasion. These sentences are true or false. Combinations of statements form arguments, which can be classified as deductive or inductive. More complex arguments, such as theories and conditional proofs, were addressed after you mastered the basic types. You learned to avoid common fallacies. Finally, you expanded your tools with Venn diagrams and syllogism rules.

All five areas—words, truth, arguments, special arguments, and fallacies—are important in every aspect of your education. After completing this study, you should recognize how useful it is. Tackle difficult concepts now while you have guidance, so you will be prepared for difficulties when no teachers are there to help. You have probably not mastered all the material in the text. You could strengthen any weak areas that you recognized when taking the final test by rereading those chapters. Now that you have a general overview of the book, many things will seem clear with a second reading. Now review a few of the benefits of logic.

First, though you may have found the symbolism, truth tables, and proofs difficult, the practice with analysis and detail has helped your reasoning skills more than you probably realize. In physical work, exercise drills strengthen muscles that may later be used in practical construction projects. So by the time you use your analytical skills in engineering, business, homemaking, or in studying biblical Greek or modern French, you may have forgotten the strengthening received from mental exercise drills in logic.

Second, it should help your objective test-taking skills. Consideration of when compound statements are true should help you correctly answer true-false questions. You also saw how multiple choice and matching questions are answered by the process of elimination—a repeated use of disjunctive syllogism (or cases). Since most people will take tests throughout life, test-taking skills are important. There are entrance tests for college and graduate school, comprehensive tests for various academic and professional degrees, proficiency tests for various abilities such as accounting and driving, and recreational tests in the form of trivia games. Perhaps you will write tests as a teacher or home educator. Tests are unavoidable; everyone at some time for some special reason must take a test.

Third, your study should help your communication skills, both oral and written. This is important not only in school but also throughout life. Every business executive writes reports; so do researchers, nurses, and doctors. Computer programmers must document their programs. Teachers and salesmen communicate all day long. In each case it is essential that you make a point clearly and give good reasons based on true statements. Each chapter provides lessons for you. In simplified form, be sure that you do the following:

1. Clarify meanings of key terms properly.
2. Check that your statements are true (go to sources; avoid hearsay).
3. Use valid deductions and strong inductions.
4. Test theories and hypothetical reasoning.
5. Avoid fallacies.

Fourth, this study should improve your listening skills. If you get into the habit of identifying main points and supportive arguments, you will get the key points when you take notes. Test the support for fallacies, but be sure you are fair to the speaker's position and keep the words in context. You don't like people nitpicking your casual comments, nor do you like people twisting your meaning. Give the benefit of doubt as much as possible. Perhaps something could have been said more clearly, but if you knew what the speaker meant, his communication was successful.

Most importantly, your study of logic helps you understand God and His Word. This benefit is eternal. You have memorized verses that show the importance of these concepts from God's perspective. Let's see if you remember your verses and why they are important. Take the matching quizzes that follow and put your test-taking skills to work. (You never know when a test may come up!)

Part One: Logic in Scripture

1. Definition   A. Matt. 22: 44-45

2. Compound sentence (emphasizes   B. I Cor. 9:9-10
   meaning of the connective "and")

3. Rule of logic (biconditional rule to   C. Heb. 11:1
   express an equivalence)

4. Inductive argument (analogy)   D. James 2:10-11

5. Deductive argument (*modus ponens*)   E. II Peter 3:3-6

6. Refutation of inductive fallacy   F. I John 5:12

Part Two: Logic Commanded and Exemplified in Scripture

1. Fallacies are common. Beware of false   A. Matt. 12:36
   reasoning!

2. Words are important. Watch your words!   B. Matt. 22:31-32

3. Truth is important. Scripture is truth!   C. John 16:13

4. Reasoning is important for spiritual   D. John 17:17
   growth. Jesus wants you to theorize!

5. Reasoning is important to spread the   E. Acts 17:2
   gospel. Paul reasoned everywhere he
   preached!

6. The Holy Spirit will help you use good   F. Col. 2:3, 8-9
   logic. Ask for His help!

We hope that you will continue to use this study. May it help you as you "Study to shew thyself approved unto God, a workman that needeth not to be ashamed, rightly dividing the word of truth" (II Tim. 2:15).

References

Carson, D. A. *Exegetical Fallacies*. Grand Rapids: Baker Book House, 1984.

Huff, Darrell. *How to Lie with Statistics*. New York: W. W. Norton & Company, 1954.

Hurley, Patrick J. *Logic*. Belmont, California: Wadsworth Publishing Company, 1988.

Read, John G. and C. L. Burdick. *Fossils, Strata and Evolution*. Culver City, California: Scientific-Technical Presentations, 1979.

Answers to Questions

Chapter 1

1. a. clarifying
   b. characterizing
   c. clarifying
   d. creating
   e. convincing
2. c
3. a. creating
   b. "that he gave his only begotten Son," clarifying
4. Words are important since (1) man is accountable for his words (Matt. 12:36), (2) God gave us the words of Scripture (II Pet. 1:21), (3) God's words are eternal (Matt. 5:18), and (4) Jesus set the example of careful use of words (Matt. 22).
5. Answers will vary.
6. Answers will vary.
7. Answers will vary.
8. Answers will vary.
9. Answers will vary.
10. Answers will vary but should include these facts: (1) Alfred North Whitehead (1861-1947) and Bertrand Russell (1872-1970) wrote (2) *Principia Mathematica* in 1913 in order (3) to prove that all math can be proved from a handful of basic rules of logic.

Chapter 2

1. a. Unrepresentative—all are North American.
   b. Poorly explained—the Philippines is an island group, not a single island.
   c. Unfamiliar
   d. Unrepresentative—all have *island* in their names.
   e. This is the best.
   f. Unrepresentative—all are in oceans, none in rivers or lakes.

2. a. neighbor
   b. kill (or murder)

3. a. classification
   b. not a definition
   c. example
   d. development
   e. synonym
   f. development
   g. not a definition

4. a. broad, encompassing rhinoceros; change *mammal* to *whale*
   b. broad, encompassing bats; narrow, excluding ostriches; change *flying* to *feathered*
   c. narrow, excluding *is, have, know;* add ''or states of being''
   d. broad, encompassing bridge collapse; add ''because of dizziness''

5. family: favor; type: unmerited; implications: (1) Grace is a favor, a gift. (2) Grace is not merited; it cannot be earned. The type distinguishes grace from merited favors such as returning an invitation to dinner.

6. The terms have different connotations, and the harder word should not be used to define the basic term.

7. Answers will vary.

8. a. Root words and word derivations do not always provide insight into word meaning.
   b. Do not read back the modern meaning of a word into ancient literature.

    c. Do not read forward an older (but not obsolete) meaning of a word into modern literature.

    d. Do not jump to conclusions without careful and thorough study of the background of words.

9. Answers will vary.

10. Answers will vary but must include that (1) Kurt Gödel (1906-78) was (2) born in Brünn, Austria (now Bruno, Czech Republic), and (3) taught at Vienna (1930-38) and Princeton (1953-76). (4) His Undecideability Theorem proved that no general logical system can be both consistent and complete. (Man will never know everything.) (5) Russell and Whitehead's goal of a complete logical system encompassing all of mathematics is therefore unattainable.

Chapter 3

1. a. exclamation   b. command   c. statement
   d. question   e. request
2. a. exclamation   b. command   c. question
   d. request   e. statement
3. a. False; some birds cannot fly.   Example: ostrich
   b. True.   Negation: No mammals fly.
   c. False; some mammals lay eggs.   Example: platypus
   d. True.   Negation: All vegetables are green.
4. a. False   b. True   c. True   d. False
   e. True   f. False   g. True
5. a. I will deny Thee.
   b. The waters did not prevail 150 days.
   c. The sun is not the only star that appears brighter than Sirius.
   d. Istanbul is not the capital of Turkey.
   e. Richard, earl of Cornwall, was a King of England from the House of York.
   f. James K. Polk was not the eleventh president of the U.S.
   g. The negation of a universal categorical is not a particular categorical.
6. a. Peter denied the Lord (Matt. 26:74-75).
   d. Ankara is the capital of Turkey.
   f. James K. Polk is the eleventh president of the U.S.
7. These groups conspired to kill Jesus, which was an evil act. Though he was evil, Caiaphas did speak the truth that Jesus would die for the nation.
8. It does *not* prove that abortion should be permitted. An example does not prove a universal. You cannot refute ''some abortions should not be permitted'' by arguing that ''some should be permitted.'' These are not negations, and both can be true.
9. If S represents the light being ''on,'' then flipping the switch to ''off'' corresponds to $\sim S$. A second flip of the switch turns it back ''on.'' In other words, $\sim(\sim S) = S$. The double negation rule applies to light switches.

10. Answers must include that (1) Chrysippus (279-206 B.C.) was (2) born in Soli, Cilicia. (3) He treated propositions as being true or false and determined truth values of compound statements from the truth values of the parts. (4) This contribution formed the basis for truth tables.

Chapter 4

1. Separate accounts permit independent use of funds. A joint OR account permits both to use all funds while trusting each other to spend wisely. A joint AND account permits both to use all funds, avoids accidental overdrafts from each writing a large check, and provides accountability to avoid hasty decisions. They will probably get a joint OR account for convenience and ability for either to take advantage of limited sales.

2. Joint OR and joint AND accounts are similar in availability of funds in that all funds are available to both parties. Separate accounts are similar to joint OR accounts in independent usage in that checks can be written without the spouse's consent. Separate accounts are similar to joint AND accounts in accountability in that no funds can leave an account without that account holder's signature.

3. a. False; T ∧ F. Roosevelt's presidency (1901-1909) included the Pure Food and Drug Act (1906) but not Prohibition (1920).

   b. True; $\sim R \wedge \sim J = T \wedge T$

   c. True; $F \rightarrow F$

   d. True; either viewpoint permits the OR to be true.

4. a. False; conifers are neither.

   b. True

   c. False; bears can, but humans get sick.

   d. False; pitcher plants also eat insects.

   e. False; some are, but some aren't.

   f. False; ferns are not flowering plants.

   g. True

   h. False; having gills is necessary for being a fish but not sufficient. An octopus (or clam, squid, tadpole) has gills, too.

5. a. conditional   b. conjunction   c. negation
   d. biconditional   e. simple   f. conjunction
   g. disjunction
6.

~	A	→	~	B
F	T	T	F	T
F	T	T	T	F
T	F	F	F	T
T	F	T	T	F

7. not an equivalence

(P	∧	Q)	↔	(P	→	~	Q)
T	T	T	F	T	F	F	T
T	F	F	F	T	T	T	F
F	F	T	F	F	T	F	T
F	F	F	F	F	T	T	F

8. a. converse

(A	→	B)	↔	(B	→	A)
T	T	T	T	T	T	T
T	F	F	F	F	T	T
F	T	T	F	T	F	F
F	T	F	T	F	T	F

b.

(B	→	A)	↔	(~	A	→	~	B)
T	T	T	T	F	T	T	F	T
F	T	T	T	F	T	T	T	F
T	F	F	T	T	F	F	F	T
F	T	F	T	T	F	T	T	F

c.

(A	→	B)	↔	(~	B	→	~	A)
T	T	T	T	F	T	T	F	T
T	F	F	T	T	F	F	F	T
F	T	T	T	F	T	T	T	F
F	T	F	T	T	F	T	T	F

9. a. 6   b. 2   c. 5   d. 1   e. 4   f. 3
10. Answers will vary but must include that (1) George Boole
    (1815-64) of Lincoln, England, wrote *The Mathematical Analy-
    sis of Logic* (1847) and *Investigation of the Laws of Thought*
    (1854). (2) He studied the operators AND, OR, and NOT, creating
    the system now called Boolean algebra. (3) His work applies to
    electrical circuits, probability, insurance, and information theory.

Chapter 5

1. a. Some plant is not a monocotyledon and not a dicotyledon.

   b. The orientation of coccus bacteria cell division is consistently in the same plane, the daughter cells remain attached, and the resulting bacterial growth is not streptococcus.

   c. Animals eat baneberries, but humans cannot.

   d. There are predatory plants besides the Venus's-flytrap.

   e. Some fungi are not saprophytic.

   f. There is a plant that does not flower or a flower that is not from a plant.

   g. *Lichen* does not mean the same as "a symbiosis between algae and a fungus."

   h. Some fish do not have gills, or some creatures with gills are not fish.

2. $(A \rightarrow B) \leftrightarrow (\sim B \rightarrow \sim A)$
   $(B \rightarrow A) \leftrightarrow (\sim A \rightarrow \sim B)$
   $(\sim A \rightarrow \sim B) \leftrightarrow (B \rightarrow A)$
   $(\sim B \rightarrow \sim A) \leftrightarrow (A \rightarrow B)$

3. $\sim S \rightarrow \sim L$, inverse

4. A biconditional asserts an implication and its converse. Since the converse and inverse are equivalent, this is the same as asserting an implication and its inverse. Since I John 5:12 asserts an implication and its inverse, it is a biconditional. Since the Scripture is also true, it is an equivalence.

5.

(P	→	Q)	↔	(Q	→	P)
T	T	T	T	T	T	T
T	F	F	F	F	T	T
F	T	T	F	T	F	F
F	T	F	T	F	T	F

6. a.

~	(A	∧	B)	↔	(~	A	∨	~	B)
F	T	T	T	T	F	T	F	F	T
T	T	F	F	T	F	T	T	T	F
T	F	F	T	T	T	F	T	F	T
T	F	F	F	T	T	F	T	T	F

b.

~	(A	→	B)	↔	(A	∧	~	B)
F	T	T	T	T	T	F	F	T
T	T	F	F	T	T	T	T	F
F	F	T	T	T	F	F	F	T
F	F	T	F	T	F	F	T	F

c.

[A	∧	(B	∨	C)]	↔	[(A	∧	B)	∨	(A	∧	C)]
T	T	T	T	T	T	T	T	T	T	T	T	T
T	T	T	T	F	T	T	T	T	T	T	F	F
T	T	F	T	T	T	T	F	F	T	T	T	T
T	F	F	F	F	T	T	F	F	F	T	F	F
F	F	T	T	T	T	F	F	T	F	F	F	T
F	F	T	T	F	T	F	F	T	F	F	F	F
F	F	F	T	T	T	F	F	F	F	F	F	T
F	F	F	F	F	T	F	F	F	F	F	F	F

d.

(A	∨	B)	↔	(B	∨	A)
T	T	T	T	T	T	T
T	T	F	T	F	T	T
F	T	T	T	T	T	F
F	F	F	T	F	F	F

e.

(P	∨	P)	↔	P
T	T	T	T	T
F	F	F	T	F

f.

[(P	∧	Q)	∧	R]	↔	[P	∧	(Q	∧	R)]
T	T	T	T	T	T	T	T	T	T	T
T	T	T	F	F	T	T	F	T	F	F
T	F	F	F	T	T	T	F	F	F	T
T	F	F	F	F	T	T	F	F	F	F
F	F	T	F	T	T	F	F	T	T	T
F	F	T	F	F	T	F	F	T	F	F
F	F	F	F	T	T	F	F	F	F	T
F	F	F	F	F	T	F	F	F	F	F

7. Answers to the proof are provided below:
   1. given
   2. Double Negation
   3. Negation of Implication
   4. Negation of Conjunction
   5. Double Negation

8. a.

1. $P \wedge Q$	1. given
2. $\sim[\sim(P \wedge Q)]$	2. Double Negation
3. $\sim[\sim P \vee \sim Q]$	3. Negation of Conjunction
4. $\sim[\sim Q \vee \sim P]$	4. Commutative Law for Disjunction (See 6d.)
5. $\sim \sim Q \wedge \sim \sim P$	5. Negation of Disjunction
6. $Q \wedge P$	6. Double Negation

b.

1. $(P \lor Q) \lor R$	1. given
2. $\sim(\sim[(P \lor Q) \lor R])$	2. Double Negation
3. $\sim[\sim(P \lor Q) \land \sim R]$	3. Negation of Disjunction
4. $\sim[(\sim P \land \sim Q) \land \sim R)$	4. Negation of Disjunction
5. $\sim[\sim P \land (\sim Q \land \sim R)]$	5. Associative Law for Conjunction (See 6f.)
6. $\sim\sim P \lor \sim(\sim Q \land \sim R)$	6. Negation of Conjunction
7. $\sim\sim P \lor (\sim\sim Q \lor \sim\sim R)$	7. Negation of Conjunction
8. $P \lor (Q \lor R)$	8. Double Negation

c.

1. $P \land P$	1. given
2. $\sim\sim(P \land P)$	2. Double Negation
3. $\sim(\sim P \lor \sim P)$	3. Negation of Conjunction
4. $\sim(\sim P)$	4. Redundancy Rule for Disjunction (See 6e.)
5. P	5. Double Negation

d.

1. $P \rightarrow (Q \rightarrow R)$	1. given
2. $\sim P \lor (Q \rightarrow R)$	2. Apply Exercise 7.
3. $\sim P \lor (\sim Q \lor R)$	3. Apply Exercise 7.
4. $(\sim P \lor \sim Q) \lor R$	4. Associative Law for Disjunction (See 8b.)
5. $\sim(P \land Q) \lor R$	5. Negation of Conjunction
6. $(P \land Q) \rightarrow R$	6. Apply Exercise 7.

9. a.

[A	∧	(B	∨	C)]	∨	[(A	∨	B)	∧	C]
T	T	T	T	T	T	T	T	T	T	T
T	T	T	T	F	T	T	T	T	F	F
T	T	F	T	T	T	T	T	F	T	T
T	F	F	F	F	F	T	T	F	F	F
F	F	T	T	T	T	F	T	T	T	T
F	F	T	T	F	F	F	T	T	F	F
F	F	F	T	T	F	F	F	F	F	T
F	F	F	F	F	F	F	F	F	F	F

The circuit is on when (1) *A, B,* and *C* are all on, (2) *A* and *B* are on, (3) *A* and *C* are on, or (4) *B* and *C* are on.

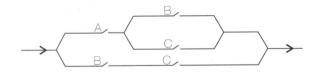

b. If X > 3 THEN IF X < > 10 THEN LET Y = 8

10. Answers will vary but must include that (1) Augustus DeMorgan (1806-71), the son of an Englishman in the East India Company, was born in Madras, India. (2) DeMorgan's famous laws apply both to logic and to sets and have been expressed in several forms. In this text they are called NC (Negation of Conjunction) and ND (Negation of Disjunction). They show the relationship between conjunctions and disjunctions under negation.

Chapter 6

1. a.

	Strong	Weak
True	Cogent	Uncogent
False	Uncogent	Uncogent

b.

	Cogent	Uncogent
Strong	True	False
Weak	Impossible	True or False

c.

	Cogent	Uncogent
True	Strong	Weak
False	Impossible	Strong or Weak

2. a. analogy   b. tendency   c. authority   d. experience

3. a. utility   b. silence   c. authority
   d. analogy   e. tendency   f. experience

4. a. All mammals bear live young.   Uncogent—weak; unrepresentative

   b. All mammals have hair.   Uncogent—weak; unrepresentative

   c. All mammals are carnivorous.   Uncogent—strong, but false premise

   d. All mammals give milk.   Cogent

5. a. There is life on other planets. (uncogent; weak appeal to experience)

   b. There is life on other planets. (uncogent; weak appeal to authority)

   c. There is no life on other planets. (cogent; appeal to authority)

   d. There is life on other planets. (uncogent; weak appeal to analogy)

e. There is life on other planets. (uncogent; strong, but has a false premise)

f. There is no life on other planets. (cogent; appeal to silence)

g. There is life on other planets. (uncogent; weak appeal to utility)

6. The subject is usually first in English sentences. Parts of speech other than the subject may be placed first in a sentence for emphasis.

7. Adverbs usually are (1) placed at the end of the sentence or (2) right before the main verb (after any helping verb). Note: If you got either of the two parts you did well. Part (1) accounts for sentences *c, d,* and *f,* and part (2) accounts for *a, b, g,* and *i.* This leaves only *e, h,* and *j.* Sentences *e* and *j* still have all adverbs last if the prepositional phrases are treated as adverbs. Apparently, the order of multiple adverbs is not very important. Sentence *h* need not be explained, since the adverb is first and is already explained by question 6 as emphatic.

8. His argument from silence is weak. Night shift workers would not be expected to pass by at noon. Most would be asleep!

9. Answers will vary. Some examples are Matthew 13:47-50, 18:10-14, 18:23-35, 20:1-16, 25:14-30; Luke 13:15-16.

10. Answers will vary but must include that (1) Peter Abelard (1079-1142) (2) defined validity in the modern sense.

Chapter 7

1. a.

[(A	→	B)	∧	(B	→	C)]	→	(A	→	C)
T	T	T	T	T	T	T	T	T	T	T
T	T	T	F	T	F	F	T	T	F	F
T	F	F	F	F	T	T	T	T	T	T
T	F	F	F	F	T	F	T	T	F	F
F	T	T	T	T	T	T	T	F	T	T
F	T	T	F	T	F	F	T	F	T	F
F	T	F	T	F	T	T	T	F	T	T
F	T	F	T	F	T	F	T	F	T	F

b.

[(A)	∧	(B)]	→	(A	∧	B)
T	T	T	T	T	T	T
T	F	F	T	T	F	F
F	F	T	T	F	F	T
F	F	F	T	F	F	F

c.

(A	∧	B)	→	A
T	T	T	T	T
T	F	F	T	T
F	F	T	T	F
F	F	F	T	F

2.

[(A	∨	B)	∧	~	A)]	→	B
T	T	T	F	F	T	T	T
T	T	F	F	F	T	T	F
F	T	T	T	T	F	T	T
F	F	F	F	T	F	T	F

3.

1.	$A \vee B$	1.	given
2.	$\sim A$	2.	given
3.	$\sim(\sim[A \vee B\,])$	3.	Double Negation
4.	$\sim(\sim A \wedge \sim B)$	4.	Negation of Disjunction
5.	$\sim(\sim[\sim A \rightarrow B])$	5.	Negation of Implication
6.	$[\sim A \rightarrow B]$	6.	Double Negation
7.	B	7.	*Modus Ponens* (premises 2 and 6)

4. Answers will vary.

5.

([~	E	→	(L	∨	G)]	∧	[~	L	∨	~	G])	→	E
F	T	T	T	T	T	**F**	F	T	F	F	T	T	T
F	T	T	T	T	F	**T**	F	T	T	T	F	T	T
F	T	T	F	T	T	**T**	T	F	T	F	T	T	T
F	T	T	F	F	F	**T**	T	F	T	T	F	T	T
T	F	T	T	T	T	**F**	F	T	F	F	T	T	F
T	F	T	T	T	F	**T**	F	T	T	T	F	F	F
T	F	T	F	T	T	**T**	T	F	T	F	T	F	F
T	F	F	F	F	F	**F**	T	F	T	T	F	T	F

The two Fs in the implication column show that it is not valid. If the word "or" in the sentence about pi (π) were changed to "and," it would be valid. The new truth table would be different in that column (only two Ts, row 4 and row 8), the bold column (only one T, row 4), and the shaded column (all T).

6.

1. $(\sim S \vee K) \rightarrow \sim E$	1. premise
2. E	2. premise
3. $\sim(\sim S \vee K)$	3. *Modus Tollens* (premises 1 and 2)
4. $S \wedge \sim K$	4. Negation of Disjunction
5. $\sim K \wedge S$	5. Commutative Law for Conjunction
6. $\sim K$	6. Simplification Argument (premise 5)
7. $E \wedge \sim K$	7. Conjunctive Syllogism (premises 2 and 6)
8. $\sim(E \rightarrow K)$	8. Negation of Implication

7. a. Transitivity Argument; valid but not sound
    b. *Modus Ponens;* valid
    c. Disjunctive Syllogism; invalid
    d. Conjunctive Syllogism; valid
    e. Simplification Argument; valid

8. a. Deductive; *Modus Tollens*
    b. Inductive; appeal to analogy
    c. Deductive; *Modus Ponens*
    d. Inductive; appeal to tendency

9. I did not call on the name of the Lord.

10. Answers will vary.

Chapter 8

1. a. consistency
   b. fruitfulness
   c. harmony with Scripture
   d. adequacy
   e. simplicity
   f. coherency
   g. accuracy

2. Fish tend to be buried lower than small animals since they live lower. Large animals tend to flee to higher ground before being trapped and so are buried higher than the small animals. Exceptions are expected because of swirling flood currents.

3. Theistic evolutionists agree that God created man (Gen. 1:27), but think that God directed the creation through evolutionary means. A few may even agree to the seven days, claiming that God used an accelerated process of evolution (Exod. 20:11). But all theistic evolutionists deny creation of man from the dust of the ground (Gen. 2:7).

4. Petrified/fossilized tree trunks have been found buried half in one rock layer and half in another that is supposedly 1,000 years different in age.

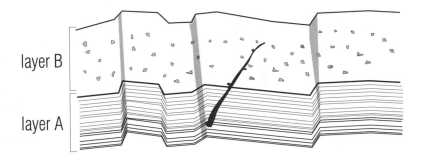

layer B

layer A

5. a. harmony with Scripture
   b. consistency; *Modus Tollens*
   c. adequacy
   d. simplicity
   e. coherency
   f. fruitfulness
   g. needing new diapers
6. Answers will vary. Discuss the following:
   a. harmony with Scripture, coherency, accuracy, or fruitfulness
   b. adequacy, accuracy, or fruitfulness
   c. adequacy, simplicity, or fruitfulness
   d. consistency with modern view of solar system, or fruitfulness.
7. Answers will vary.
8. Answers will vary. Any three points can be argued, and sample reasons are provided for each point.
   (1) Scripture does not harmonize with Hinduism, since the Bible denies reincarnation (Heb. 9:27), condemns worship of many gods (Exod. 20:3), and refutes emanational creation by showing God's creation *ex nihilo* (Gen. 1).
   (2) Hinduism, in its extreme form, views creation as being God (monism), since each emanation is a manifestation of God. Thus, all is illusory—except God. This is incoherent because the proponent who claims this is also an illusion. It is inconsistent for people to make the absolute claim that all is illusion. How can the claim itself be other than illusion, or how could anyone know?
   (3) Hinduism is inadequate to explain either the seeming reality of experience or the reason for pain and suffering.
   (4) To avoid the problem in (2), an elaborate system of emanations is sometimes used. This system fails the test of simplicity.
   (5) That Hinduism fails the test of fruitfulness is clear from its history. Neither the sciences, technology, mathematics, nor the arts have flourished where Hinduism is predominant because of the hopelessness of the systems of caste, karma (good works and merits), and reincarnation.

9. Ockham's razor is the idea that "entities should not be multi-plied needlessly." In other words, do not make things unnec-essarily complicated. In our study of theories, this is equivalent to the criterion of simplicity.

10. Answers will vary, but students know now how to make a main point and support it. The facts below should be incorpo-rated into the point. William of Ockham (1285-1349) was born at Ockham, England. He taught theology and philoso-phy at Oxford and extensively studied forms of syllogisms, classifying them as valid or invalid. He developed terminol-ogy for discussing logic and explored modal logic. He also is responsible for Ockham's razor.

Chapter 9

1. a. Law of Cases
   b. Law of Contradiction
   c. Law of Cases

2. a. Law of Deduction
   b. Law of Contradiction

3. a. Examples of matter that are good: original creation (Gen. 1:31), the man Jesus (Heb. 4:15), and all God's creatures (I Tim. 4:4)
   b. Examples of spirits that are evil: demons and Satan (II Thess. 2:8-10)
   c. Example of resurrection: Jesus Christ (Matt. 28, Mark 16, Luke 24, John 20, I Cor. 15:3-20)

4. The missing reasons are as follows:
   3. Negation of Conjunction
   4. assumed for Law of Contradiction
   5. Simplification Argument (premise 1)
   6. Simplification Argument (premise 1)
   7. Simplification Argument (premise 4)
   8. Simplification Argument (premise 4)
   9. *Modus Ponens* (premises 5, 7)
   10. *Modus Ponens* (premises 6, 8)
   11. Conjunctive Syllogism (premises 9, 10)
   12. Law of Contradiction (Step 11 and step 3 contradict, so step 4 is false.)
   13. Negation of Conjunction

5.

A	$\lor$	$\sim$	A
T	T	F	T
F	T	T	F

6.

A	$\land$	$\sim$	A
T	F	F	T
F	F	T	F

7. a.

1. $A \rightarrow C$	1. premise
2. $B \rightarrow C$	2. premise
3. $\sim\sim(A \rightarrow C)$	3. Double Negation, 1
4. $\sim(A \wedge \sim C)$	4. Negation of Implication, 3
5. $\sim A \vee C$	5. Negation of Conjunction, 4
6. $\sim\sim(B \rightarrow C)$	6. Double Negation, 2
7. $\sim(B \wedge \sim C)$	7. Negation of Implication, 6
8. $\sim B \vee C$	8. Negation of Conjunction, 7
9. $(\sim A \vee C) \wedge (\sim B \vee C)$	9. Conjunctive Syllogism, 5, 8
10. $(C \vee \sim A) \wedge (C \vee \sim B)$	10. Commutative Law for Disjunction (twice), 9
11. $C \vee (\sim A \wedge \sim B)$	11. Distribution of Disjunction, 10
12. $C \vee [\sim(A \vee B)]$	12. Negation of Disjunction, 11
13. $[\sim(A \vee B)] \vee C$	13. Commutative Law for Disjunction, 12
14. $\sim[(A \vee B) \wedge \sim C]$	14. Negation of Conjunction, 13
15. $\sim[\sim((A \vee B) \rightarrow C)]$	15. Negation of Implication, 14
16. $(A \vee B) \rightarrow C$	16. Double Negation, 15

b.

1.	$A \rightarrow C$	1.	premise
2.	$B \rightarrow C$	2.	premise
3.	$(A \rightarrow C) \wedge (B \rightarrow C)$	3.	Conjunctive Syllogism, 1, 2
	4. $A \vee B$		4. assume for Law of Deduction
	5. $C \vee C$		5. Constructive Dilemma, 3, 4
	6. C		6. Redundancy Rule for Disjunction, 5
7.	$(A \vee B) \rightarrow C$	7.	Law of Deduction, 4-6

c.

1.	$A \rightarrow C$	1.	premise
2.	$B \rightarrow C$	2.	premise
3.	$(A \rightarrow C) \wedge (B \rightarrow C)$	3.	Conjunctive Syllogism, 1, 2
	4. $\sim[(A \vee B) \rightarrow C]$		4. assume for Law of Contradiction
	5. $(A \vee B) \wedge \sim C$		5. Negation of Implication
	6. $A \vee B$		6. Simplification Argument, 5
	7. $\sim C$		7. Simplification Argument (and commute), 5
	8. $C \vee C$		8. Constructive Dilemma, 3, 6
	9. C		9. Redundancy Rule for Disjunction, 8
	10. $\sim C \wedge C$		10. Conjunctive Syllogism, 7, 9
11.	$(A \vee B) \rightarrow C$	11.	Law of Contradiction, 4-10

The easiest method was the Law of Deduction.

8. a.

[(A	→	B)	∧	(~	A	→	B)]	→	B
T	T	T	**T**	F	T	T	T	T	T
T	F	F	**F**	F	T	T	F	T	F
F	T	T	**T**	T	F	T	T	T	T
F	T	F	**F**	T	F	F	F	T	F

b.

[(A	→	B)	∧	(A	→	~	B)]	→	~	A
T	T	T	**F**	T	F	F	T	T	F	T
T	F	F	**F**	T	T	T	F	T	F	T
F	T	T	**T**	F	T	F	T	T	T	F
F	T	F	**T**	F	T	T	F	T	T	F

9. Answers will vary.
10. Answers will vary but should argue a main point and include the following facts: (1) Gottfried Wilhelm von Leibniz (1646-1716) is called (2) the Father of Symbolic Logic for his application of symbols to represent and analyze logical arguments in all fields of knowledge.

Chapter 10

1. (1) C   (2) A   (3) D   (4) B
2. Answers will vary.
3. Answers will vary.
4. Answers will vary.
5. a. Argument against the person
   b. False cause (Personality types are descriptive classes at best and cannot excuse sin.)
   c. Hasty generalization (The sample is quite small and anything but random.)
   d. Strained analogy (In the face of higher costs, they should be planning on reduced profits!)
   e. Missing the point (If all commodities—vegetables of every kind, gas, lighting, rent, etc.—increased 4%, the overall cost of living increase is 4%. These percents cannot be added. His raise is probably more than the cost of living if his concern is only about a few vegetables when his rent and other commodities, such as meats, did not go up. His raise was either very generous or compensating for previous cost increases.)
   f. Suppressed evidence (The error estimate on the best of IQ tests is at least ± 3%. A difference of only three points is not significant; the boys are equally smart.)
6. (1) D   (2) B   (3) E   (4) A   (5) C
7. (1) D   (2) D   (3) H   (4) B   (5) I
8. a. Weak—false cause
   b. Strong—appeal to tendency
   c. Weak—missing the point (A pay raise of 20% is computed on the smaller and does not restore the original. A 20% decrease from $100 is $80, but a 20% increase from $80 is only $96.)
   d. Strong—appeal to authority
   e. Weak—exceptional experience
   f. Strong—appeal to utility (Quality of work is a condition of job security.)
   g. Weak—appeal to force

h. Weak—red herring (The subject changed from choices to a need for diligence. Daniel had no choice. Daniel's case proves that God is sovereign over our circumstances and works events out for our good. But Daniel 6:10 shows that Daniel's heart was toward Jerusalem and his spiritual heritage, and he would have preferred studying there in the synagogues. We should desire Christian training, and Ephesians 6:4 shows that parents need to provide for such training. See II Tim. 2:15, Deut. 6:7-15, and Col. 2:3, 8).

i. Strong—argument from experience

j. Weak—argument against the person

9. A weak induction is a misuse of a proper method of induction. Twisting evidence appears to use a proper method of induction but distorts either the information or the context. In contrast, the emotional appeal does not even begin with a proper method of induction but substitutes emotion.

10. Answers will vary but should argue a main point and include these facts: (1) John Stuart Mill (1806-73) (2) explained five methods for discovering causal relations. (3) These methods expose false causes and hasty generalizations.

Chapter 11

1.

[(A	→	B)	∧	~	A]	→	~	B
T	T	T	F	F	T	T	F	T
T	F	F	F	F	T	T	T	F
F	T	T	T	T	F	F	F	T
F	T	F	T	T	F	T	T	F

2. (1) B (2) D (3) C (4) A

3. Answers will vary.

4. (1) C (2) E (3) F (4) B (5) A

5. a. improper negation
   b. denying the antecedent
   c. affirming the consequent

6. The fallacy is formal because it changes the form of the transitivity argument, replacing the premise $B \to C$ with its converse $C \to B$. It is a reversed conditional fallacy.

7. The premise means that the chapter discusses types of errors. The conclusion takes "in this chapter" as modifying "errors" (rather than "warned") and interprets the premises as, "Be careful when you read this error-ridden material." The equivocation is based on the grammatical interpretation of "in this chapter." The equivocation, however, was unintentional, caused by misunderstanding the premise. (Amphiboly typically occurs as an unintentional equivocation based on a possible but unlikely misreading of a statement. Because the reading is often unlikely, it will usually be humorous to the onlooker.)

8. Begging the question—trick question variety

9. Answers will vary.

10. Answers will vary but must present and defend a main point. Include that Gottlob Frege (1848-1925) wrote *Begriffsschrift,* which presents quantifiers and quantification.

Chapter 12

1. a. C b. A c. B
2. Invalid; commits the fallacies of undistributed middle, illicit major, and negative conclusion
3.

[(A	→	B)	∧	(C	→	B)]	→	(A	→	C)
T	T	T	T	T	T	T	T	T	T	T
T	T	T	T	F	T	T	F	T	F	F
T	F	F	F	T	F	F	T	T	T	T
T	F	F	F	F	T	F	T	T	F	F
F	T	T	T	T	T	T	T	F	T	T
F	T	T	T	F	T	T	T	F	T	F
F	T	F	F	T	F	F	T	F	T	T
F	T	F	T	F	T	F	T	F	T	F

4.

[(A	→	B)	∧	(A	→	C)]	→	(B	→	C)
T	T	T	T	T	T	T	T	T	T	T
T	T	T	F	T	F	F	T	T	F	F
T	F	F	F	T	T	T	T	F	T	T
T	F	F	F	T	F	F	T	F	T	F
F	T	T	T	F	T	T	T	T	T	T
F	T	T	T	F	T	F	F	T	F	F
F	T	F	T	F	T	T	T	F	T	T
F	T	F	T	F	T	F	T	F	T	F

5. Some athletes are not cows.

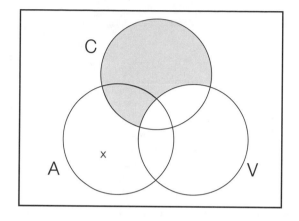

6. Some Christians are professionals.

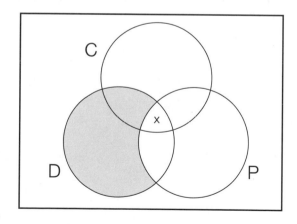

7. No chess pieces are kings.

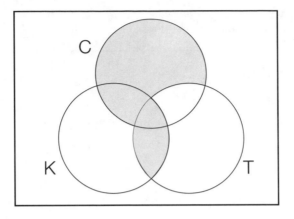

8. (1) UG   (2) UI   (3) EIF   (4) EG   (5) EI   (6) UGF
   (Note: There is no such thing as EGF or UIF. If you used
   either as an answer, reread the chapter.)
9. (1) C   (2) B   (3) I   (4) B   (5) G   (6) H   (7) F
10. Answers will vary but should properly argue a main point
    and mention that John Venn (1834-1923) developed the Venn
    diagrams.

Answers to Review Questions

1. (16 points—4 points each) (1) D (2) A (3) C (4) B
2. (20 points—4 points each) (1) C (2) A (3) D (4) B (5) C
3. (15 points—3 points each) (1) E (2) A (3) C (4) D (5) B
4. (20 points—10 points each table)

a.

(A	∨	B)	∧	(A	→	B)
T	T	T	T	T	T	T
T	T	F	F	T	F	F
F	T	T	T	F	T	T
F	F	F	F	F	T	F

b.

(A	↔	B)	→	~	(A	∧	B)
T	T	T	F	F	T	T	T
T	F	F	T	T	T	F	F
F	F	T	T	T	F	F	T
F	T	F	T	T	F	F	F

5. (16 points—2 points each)
   (1) D (2) H (3) F (or B) (4) G (5) J (6) B (or F)
   (7) I (8) A
6. (20 points—4 points each) (1) F (2) A (3) D (4) B (5) C
7. (20 points—4 points each) (1) D (2) A (3) C (4) G (5) B
8. (28 points—4 points each) (1) A (2) C (3) G (4) E (5) B
   (6) D, conflicts with Second Law of Thermodynamics (7) F
9. (16 points—4 points each) (1) C (2) A (3) D (4) B
10. (24 points—2 points each)
    (1) G (2) C (3) E (4) A (5) F (6) I
    (7) A (8) D (9) A (10) L (11) M
    (12) J (The best answers would be amphiboly or equivoca-
    tion, but those are not options.)
11. (20 points—2 points each)
    (1) E (2) L (3) H (4) C (5) B
    (6) J (7) A (8) K (9) P (10) F

12. (12 points—3 points each)
  a.

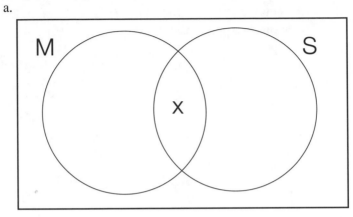

  b. All forests are photogenic (places).

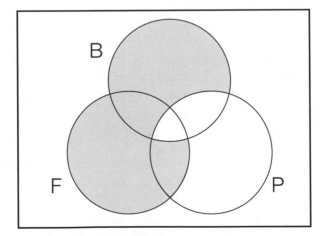

c. No streams are oceans.

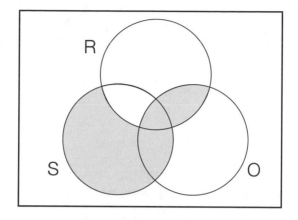

d. Some mountainous places are not boring.

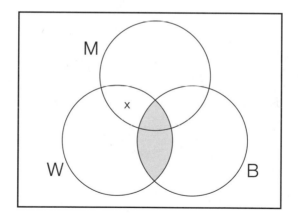

13. (20 points—4 points each) (1) F (2) E (3) B (4) G (5) D
14. Part A (12 points—2 points each blank)
   3. SA, 2

   5. ~B

   6. A → B   6. DS, 1, 3

   7. ~A   7. MT, 5, 6

   Part B (10 points—2 points each)
    6. TA, 2, 3
    7. AA, 4
    8. MP, 1, 7
    9. CS, 6, 8
    10. CD, 5, 9
15. Part A (12 points—2 points each)
    4. MP, 1, 3
    5. SA, 3
    6. CS, 4, 5
    7. MP, 2, 6
    8. Law of Deduction, 3–7
    9. Commutative Law for Conjunction, 8
   Part B (18 points—2 points each)
    3. assume
    4. NC, 3
    5. DC, 1
    6. SA, 5
    7. DN, 6
    8. DS, 4, 7
    9. MP, 2, 6
    10. CS, 8, 9
    11. Law of Contradiction, 3–10
16. (1 point) Answers will vary.

Afterword

Part One
    1. C   2. D   3. F   4. B   5. A   6. E
Part Two
    1. F   2. A   3. D   4. B   5. E   6. C

Scripture Index

221

Memory Verses

INDEX